ANTIQUAIRES

To Raphaël

© Assouline
601 West 26th Street New York 10001 NY
www.assouline.com

© Photographs Laziz Hamani/Éditions Assouline, Paris.

Graphic design: Isabelle Ducat

Translated from the French by
Josephine Bacon, Alexis Duclos and Claudine Vignon
Adaptation: Brigitte de Roquemaurel

Color separation: Gravor (Switzerland)
Printed and bound by Canale (Italy)

ISBN: 2 84323 213 9

Front cover: FRÉMONTIER. Neo-Renaissance table by Lebois.
Bacchus in white marble by Ludovico Salvetti. Bust of
Julius Caesar, Roman head of the 3rd century, draped
clothes added in the 18th century.
Back cover: WATELET. A pair of plaster floor lamps by Serge
Roche (c. 1934) and a *tête-à-tête* seat by Jansen (c. 1945).

PHOTOGRAPHS LAZIZ HAMANI

ANTIQUAIRES

THE FINEST ANTIQUE DEALERS IN PARIS

JEAN-LOUIS GAILLEMIN

ASSOULINE

CONTENTS

**GALLERY
PATRICK FOURTIN**
Study of face,
circa 1935.
Original terra cotta
by Bizette Lindet.

PREFACE

From the *friperie* merchant and upholsterer of the Ancien Régime to today's dealers in antiques and second-hand furniture, *via* the Old Curiosity Shop and Balzac's *Cousin Pons,* antique dealers remain above all intermediaries, the middlemen between the collector and the past. They are magicians who cast a spell upon the detritus of times past, turning them into treasure trove; the priests of a religion which has its own temples and chapels. They trade in relics which may range from a marquetry *bonheur-du-jour* by Topino to a schoolboy's desk by Jean Prouvé. After such objects have done their time in the purgatory into which everything that is no longer fashionable is consigned, the dealer rediscovers them, nurtures them, and gives them new life. In this respect, he is an inventor. It hardly matters whether the material is gold or steel, porcelain or formica: each item revived through the perceptiveness of the few is snatched from its original purpose to become the vehicle for fantasies.

Each era has its own. Renaissance princes dreamed of the Roman Empire whose magnificence they sought to revive, as they filled their curio cabinets with medals, *intaglios,* and busts from Antiquity. The French Revolution caused such an upheaval in Europe that, only a few years later, rich English collectors, led by the Prince Regent–the future George IV–were picking over the remains of the Ancien Régime, a movement which grew in the aftermath of the Napoleonic Wars. King Louis-Philippe subsequently refurnished Versailles and the empress Eugenie surrounded herself with souvenirs of Marie-Antoinette. The new rich, the wealthy European and American financiers dreamed, in their turn, of becoming Renaissance princes. These two forms of collector's delirium, "18th century" and "High Curiosity," lasted until 1900, at which time modern styles succeeded each other rapidly, dragging new forms of nostalgia in their wake. The French Empire and Restoration were rediscovered by the contemporaries of Art Deco, then the unbridled Baroque and the Napoleon III styles became fashionable again in the 1930s. About this time, African and Polynesian art and archeological excavated objects were added to Chinese, Turkish and Japanese curios of former times.

Since World War II, the movement has gained momentum and the objects' purgatory has significantly decreased in length. In the 1960s, Sarah Bernhardt's taste was all the rage, in 1970, people emulated Jacques Doucet, and in the 1980s, the white drawing room of Charles and Marie-Laure de Noailles, at their home on the Place des États-Unis, had the same prestige for young dealers that Marie-Antoinette's couch had for Pierre de Nolhac. Today, a few rusty tubes by Eileen Gray arouse as much excitement among American traders as a chalice by Cellini did for the late Pierpont Morgan. Already, work by Starck can be found in the flea markets, alongside plastic incunabula.

It is quite a challenge to evoke the Parisian antique dealers and their history. The owners of modern art galleries who monitor the work of their artists are actors of the history of art, but antique dealers, like collectors, create the history of taste, a history that is more subtle and more discreet. While the collectors may sometimes allow a peep inside their doors, antique dealers are a more secretive lot. Very little has been written about them, and their memoirs are more anecdotal than useful. Their stock is ephemeral by definition and even their large numbers discourage the would-be chronicler.

The author of this book is thus very conscious of the gaps in this work and the choices he was forced to make. Priority has been given to "general" dealers who combine objects, furnishings, paintings and sculptures, to the detriment of the specialists, including dealers of ancient and modern paintings. Given the growing number of dealers in the 20th century and their importance, this book is voluntarily limited in scope: rather than present an exhaustive guide, the author has prefered a more in-depth illustrated study of a selection of dealers.

CHAPTER 1

ORIGINS OF AN OCCUPATION:
ANTIQUE DEALER

FROM OLD CURIOSITY SHOP TO ANTIQUE DEALERS

It was not until 1865 that the word "antiquaire" was first used in the modern sense of a "dealer in valuable old objects." The word "antiquarian" once meant what "archeologist" does today, and by extension indicated someone who was an expert in or a connoisseur of ancient relics. Yet the occupation of dealer in works of art, curiosities, and ancient relics has existed since the Middle Ages. Goldsmiths were no doubt the first of these advisors, middlemen, and dealers in old works of art, acting surreptitiously on behalf of the great and the good, the French aristocracy, to enrich the treasuries of princes and prelates. At the same time, a select group of collectors, art-lovers, and brokers began to seek out old artefacts in the little boutiques huddled around the cathedral of Notre-Dame in Paris, where illuminators, goldsmiths, and cabinet-makers plied their trade and also dealt in second-hand items. At the same time, however, there were the *brocanteurs,* dealers in used goods who belonged to the guild of *fripiers* (old clothes and objects dealers), an important branch of Parisian trade from the 18th century. Their official occupation was restricted to the "purchase, sale, and restoration of old objects." Their operations were strictly controlled, due to the fact that they were particularly prone to engage in passing off fakes and forgeries and deal in stolen goods. Even at this early stage, there were two classes of such dealers, those who owned a store and the itinerant hawkers. However, by 1188, all the *fripiers* were allowed to display their finds and their old clothes on a Parisian square located near the Cemetery of the Innocents.

From the 16th century onwards, Italy gave new meaning to the trade in antiques. Antiquaries and collectors first appeared in northern Italy, especially in Venice and Florence. A brisk trade developed in marble statues, fragments of ancient monuments, stone carvings, and inscriptions recently unearthed in archeological digs. The collectors became more knowledgeable and sought rarities, the unusual and the authentic. Thus, alongside the trade in valuable objects, there developed a trade in collectibles, and curio cabinets gradually replaced the treasuries of the wealthy. This trade developed throughout the Renaissance, though it still had little in common with the modern market. At the time, it was a huge yet unorganized trade in artefacts which circulated freely throughout Europe and the dealers, usually acting on behalf of a prince, were simply intermediaries.

AUCTION SALE
Popular engraving by Clément, showing an improvised sale on a streetcorner, 1796. Private collection.

À LA TESTE NOIRE
Publicity card of Périer,
ironmonger, quai de la Mégisserie,
engraved by Gabriel de St. Aubin,
1767. Private collection.

In the 16th century, these merchants began to open booths in Paris along the banks of the Seine at the Quai de la Mégisserie, which eventually became one of the main centers of the Parisian antiques trade. According to Gilles Corrozet, "In the year one thousand five hundred and fifty, in the month of August, there were several pictures sold in the Mégisserie, altar tables, paintings, and other church adornments, which had been brought over and saved from churches in England." By the end of the century, the trade in art had become large enough to arouse the interest of a tax collector named Barthélémy de Laffémas, controller-general of trade in France, who considered taxing valuable collectors' items entering France and banning anything made more than fifty years previously. However, neither Italy and France were yet endowed with institutions capable of maintaining an open market in which price comparisons might be possible and in which open competition between buyers would be the rule. In northern Europe, on the other hand, in the United Provinces, now known as the Netherlands, in Amsterdam, Leyden, and Haarlem, the first auctions were held at the very beginning of the 17th century and their popularity increased in the course of the 18th century. They were regulated in a practical and consistent manner, and gave the European art market a structure. First of all, they were granted a single, central location, the old Heer Logement in Amsterdam, and to circumvent any potential interference by the guilds, an official commissioner, called the *vendu-meester* or *afslager,* was appointed by the mayor. This commissioner presided over auctions and was the judge in disputes, and a special broker was appointed to value those items that were up for sale. From 1616, the sales were often accompanied by a printed catalogue which was a way of publicizing the sale and letting even the exclusive circle of Parisian collectors know what was on offer. It is thus to the pragmatic, businesslike good sense of the Dutch that we owe the first commercial organization of the antiques trade and perhaps the origin of the French word used to describe it–*brocanteur.* The term is of obscure origin, but may be related to the Dutch word "*brok*" which means "piece, fragment," thus indicating broken objects or incomplete, mismatched sets. Once the bitter wars of the 16th century were over, in the 1620s, the merchants of Paris made regular trips to the United Provinces to buy stock for their stores, bringing back natural and oriental curiosities, paintings and prints. This is mentioned for the first time in the Livre Commode, for the year 1692, a sort of trade directory of the period, which includes "sellers of curiosities and jewelry."

In the 18th century, commerce in France was still based on the guild system which required the members of each guild to pursue no trade or profession other than that defined in the statutes of his corporation. The reality was more complex, however. The prerogatives of the sellers of second-hand clothes (*fripiers*) were shared by the drapers (*marchands merciers*), the upholsterers (*marchands tapissiers*), and certain skilled painters, all of whom dealt in second-hand goods in one way or another. Their little stores were as popular for their old curiosities as for modern works of art, imported items, and luxury craftsmanship.

THE "FRIPIERS BROCANTEURS"

The largest group of dealers were the *fripiers brocanteurs* who maintained their right throughout the century to "sell and buy, barter and exchange all sorts of furniture, apparel, linen, upholstery, fabrics, lace, upholstery and decorative braiding, muffs, furs, worked pelts, hats, belts, swords, spurs, shoulder straps, leather, brass, iron, old bales of feathers, new and old woodwork, and all sorts of merchandise, old and new and unclaimed." In 1776, there were some serious disruptions to the trade, when Turgot, Louis XVI's Minister of Finance, declared the occupation to be open, although second-hand goods dealers continued to be attached to two other guilds. Those who dealt mainly in old clothes were classified as tailors and those who specialized in second-hand furniture became members of the upholsterers' guild. These changes did not, however, force the dealers to abandon the stores they had opened around the Temple district and under the pillars of the Halles, the central market of Paris, to which they had moved a few centuries previously. The area was frequented for its undeniably picturesque setting right up until the French Revolution.

Trade in second-hand goods continued to flourish in the streets. It was run mainly by women. These were the wives and daughters of impoverished crafts-men, who were known as *crieuses de vieux chapeaux* (old hat hawkers.) These women would buy goods privately and at public auctions of furniture, clothing, and other items which they usually sold on to the merchants in the Halles, although the men considered the intervention of the women to be overpaid. The

SECOND-HAND DEALER WOMAN GETTING DRESSED
Engraving from a popular book of the middle of the 19th century.

women street-traders belonged to no collective body but adopted their own trade practices and had their own form of self-regulation. For instance, they never bid against each other at auctions so as not to push the prices up at each other's expense. On the contrary, they would form a dealers' ring and after the auction closed would proceed to "view the lots," in other words to set new prices for those items which certain of their number greatly desired, raffling off the rest among themselves. The women dealers would meet every Monday at the Foire de l'Esprit, a fair held at the Place de Grève, and display their wares. Although they were ignorant of the true value of what they were selling, they cried their wares "with gusto."

THE UPHOLSTERERS, THE "MARCHANDS TAPISSIERS"

Thanks to their dual occupation of craftsman and merchant, the upholsterers gradually became the main furniture-sellers in France. Of course, their wares consisted of new furniture carefully upholstered by the craftsmen themselves, but there was also what was known as "chance" furniture, that is to say second-hand items. Thanks to their extensive knowledge of their craft, they were always able to spot quality furniture and many aristocrats and members of the upper classes relied on their judgment. It is no surprise to find the names of the best-known upholsterers and furniture-makers in the margins of sales catalogues where they are listed as the buyers.

Most of the upholsterers plied their trade in the Bonne-Nouvelle district, near the Rue de Cléry, close to the car-

pentry workshops. One of these was Antoine Godefroy, who held the warrant of upholsterer from Madame de Pompadour and her brother, the marquis of Marigny. Other dealers, however, preferred to move closer to their clientele, and opened stores in the elegant neighborhoods. They included François Labite, supplier to Madame du Barry, and Dubuquoy, "merchant upholsterer in ordinary to Monseigneur le Dauphin," whose premises were in the highly fashionable Rue du Faubourg-Saint-Honoré.

THE DRAPERS, THE "MARCHANDS MERCIERS"

In the 18th century, by far the most important guild was that of the drapers. It covered such a huge range of occupations that its members were subdivided into twenty different classes. The skinners, mirror-makers, and ironmongers belonged to the main body of drapers, as did specialists in curiosities and sellers of paintings who together formed the thirteenth class of drapery. In his *Dictionnaire du Commerce*, Savary de Brustolon defines their activities as "dealing in all sorts of little curios which serve to adorn persons or apartments" and mentions several types of wares one might encounter in their stores: "prints, candelabra, sconces, gilt, copper or bronze candlesticks, crystal chandeliers, bronzes, marble statues, and wooden figurines and those made of other materials; longcase clocks, timepieces, and watches; cabinets, coffers, closets, tables, shelves, wooden and gilded pedestal tables and side-tables, marble tables, & other merchandise & curiosities suitable for the decoration of homes."

These members of the drapers' guild specialized in small objects and fashionable furniture. The shrewdest among them could sense trends and even set new fashions. In order to satisfy a clientele that was always hungry for

novelties, they would perform ingenious restorations, thus enhancing the value of the objects they imported or bought, transforming them into genuine art objects. The drapers-cum-antique dealers sought oriental art of the classic periods, Chinese bronzes, Tang' ceramics, and antique lacquerware. They were tireless travellers, combing the United Provinces and, like the famous Gersaint, looking for "unusual porcelain, little cabinets, boxes and other objects covered in ancient Chinese lacquer."

All these exotic or ancient objects were rarely displayed in the draper's shop without having first been subjected to a certain amount of restoration. The lacquer veneer on screens, boxes, and cabinets was removed from its original backing in order to be applied to a bureau, commode, or pair of corner-cabinets made by skilled Parisian cabinet-makers such as Bernard Van Risen Burgh (B.V.R.B.), Martin Carlin, or Adam Weisweiller.

In the 1770s, Claude-François Julliot was one of those who had the great good fortune to purchase at public auction, for a very low price, furniture made a century earlier by the famous André-Charles Boulle, cabinet-maker to King Louis XIV. He hired the services of master craftsmen Étienne Levasseur, Philippe-Claude Montigny, René Dubois, Joseph Baumhauer, and Adam Weisweiller to make copies of this furniture, and to restore or modify it, so that he could sell it at a much higher price to his wealthy, aristocratic clientele. The enthusiasm engendered by this remade version of Boulle furniture encouraged Philippe-François Julliot, son of Claude-François, to apply this audacious and lucrative idea to furniture inlaid with pietra dura, which had also been fashionable in the late 17th century. The drapers were also skilled at enhancing oriental porcelain, soapstone, carved shells and coral with ormolu mountings. They employed the greatest engravers of the period, Caffiéri, Duplessi, and Gouthière, to do this work. The result was some of the most exquisite Parisian fantasy pieces of the 18th century.

This specialized aspect of the trade was practiced by several Parisian curiosity dealers. Their stores, always pleasant and well-stocked, lined the Rue de la Monnaie, the Quai de Conti, and the Quai de la Mégisserie from the early years of the century. In the Rue de la Monnaie, crowds flocked to Darnault at the sign of *Au Roy d'Espagne* and Louis XV's goldsmith and jeweler, Lazare Duvaux, was equally popular. To discover the treasures on offer at Thomas-Joachim Hébert's *Écu de France,* one had to visit the Quai de la Mégisserie, and continue in the same direction to the Quai Conti to inspect Charles-Raymond Grancher's shop *Au Petit Dunkerque.* François-Edmé Gersaint was a friend of the artist Watteau, who painted the store sign for *À la Pagode,* his store on Notre-Dame Bridge. Good publicity was ensured by a tradecard drawn by François Boucher and by announcements like the following which appeared in the *Mercure de France* newspaper: "Le Sieur Gersaint, merchant, Notre-Dame Bridge, who for several years has been travelling in order to collect rare items and all types of curiosities, recently returned to Paris with a considerable collection of unique pieces (…) pagodas and other works of rare beauty from old Japan, mobile and non-mobile figurines from India, of a very singular nature and admirable design."

The Rue Saint-Honoré and the adjacent streets became the fashionable district in the mid-18th century. At that time, the most elegant clientele in Paris would meet at *Au Chagrin de Turquie,* Lazare Duvaux's new boutique. Between 1748 and 1758, Madame de Pompadour spent the astronomical sum of 376,000 livres at this antique dealer's. Wealthy clientele also helped make the fortunes of Simon de la Hoguette and of Jean Dulac. *À la Couronne d'Or,* owned by Simon-Philippe Poirier, who was later succeeded by Dominique Daguerre and Lignereux, was another great attraction where one could buy unusual small pieces of furniture adorned with Sèvres porcelain plaques and other outrageously expensive baubles. "I do not dare," wrote Thérmidore, "go near Hébert's door; he always manages to sell me a thousand items against my will. He has been the ruination of many. He does in France what the French do in America: he exchanges trinkets for gold bars." Claude-François Julliot Fils was in the Rue du Four, on the corner of the Rue Saint-Honoré, under the sign *Aux Curieux des Indes.*

À LA PAGODE
Gersaint's publicity card, drawn by François Boucher, 1740.

THE GREAT AUCTIONS AND THE EXPERT DEALER

The great auctions of the second half of the 18th century were an opportunity for dealers to prove themselves indispensable experts and brokers. It is they who took upon themselves the risk of stocking worthy but unfashionable merchandise. The first series of auctions was held at the Tuileries Palace by the Royal Furniture Custodian himself, who wanted to make more room and fill his coffers at the same time. In 1741, during the reign of Louis XV, quantities of fabrics, furniture, chairs, and lacquered items were valued by Boissé, the upholsterer, furnisher of the king, Gaudreau, the cabinet-maker, and by Julliot. Drapers, upholsterers, *fripiers* and individual collectors attended the auctions. Julliot purchased Cardinal Mazarin's great octagonal table inlaid with marble and pietra dura. At the 1751 sale, 24 ebony or Boulle marquetry cabinets and other items of furniture were put up for auction and bought by the same dealers and professionals. Lazare Duvaux found a cedarwood cabinet decorated with a portrait of King Henri IV on horseback, while Lemaignan acquired two cabinets inlaid with pietra dura and ormolus made by Domenico Cucci for Louis XIV. In the following year, there was a sale featuring items of semi-precious stone, lacquer and porcelain which monopolized the attention of enthusiasts for more than a month and made the fortunes of the most important drapers. As an example, an antique cameo vase entitled *Apollo and*

**CHEST OF DRAWERS
BY MARTIN CARLIN**
At the sale after the death of
the Duke d'Aumont, Darnault
bought two ancient Japanese
lacquer cabinets. Three years later,
the draper (*marchand mercier*)
asked the cabinet-maker Martin
Carlin to use the lacquer from
the cabinets to decorate another
chest of drawers. The new piece
of furniture was subsequently
delivered to the royal castle of
Bellevue. Louvre Museum, Paris.

Diana, from Louis XIV's collection, sold for 434 livres to Jean-Baptiste-Pierre Lebrun before it was acquired by Jacques Guay, the engraver. All of these sales contributed to increasing the number of items of "chance merchandise" and expanding the taste for curios.

Another series of auctions was held in 1760 and, by the 1780s, such sales were held as frequently as once a week. They were organized by a few merchants in the Rue Saint-Honoré under a committee of auctioneer-valuers who fulfilled the same functions as today's auctioneer-valuers. The activity of the merchants moved to the auction rooms which they arranged to have opened near their stores. In the late 1770s, a crowd of onlookers and collectors jostled at the Hôtel d'Aligre and the old Hôtel de Bullion in the Rue Saint-Honoré, where Alexandre-Joseph Paillet and Lebrun, "a dealer and valuer of paintings and all sorts of curiosities," organized and directed the dispersion of the most important collections of the Ancien Régime. On the very eve of the Revolution, this small world made tracks for 96, Rue de Cléry to follow Lebrun to his new auction rooms.

The trade, of which records survive in the printed catalogues produced under the egis of the dealers themselves, encouraged them to improve and extend their knowledge of art history and expertise in antiques. At the sales, they acted mainly as middlemen, in exchange for a commission of between three and four percent. The queen herself instructed P. F. Julliot to purchase, at the sale held after the demise of the Duke d'Aumont in December, 1782, two exceptional carved porphyry tables made by the craftsman Gouthière and a very valuable round bowl in flowered jasper. At the same sale, Paillet was instructed by the king to purchase various objects and paintings from the Duke of Chabot, Richelieu, and other eminent people. Despite these examples, paintings monopolized the activity of most of the dealers of the period, although a few, including Claude-François Julliot or Milliotti, were already specialized in the authentification and sale of objects and furniture.

In addition to the professional dealers, there were a few individuals who sought to act alone, but the known brokers and merchants saw this as an intrusion and a curb on their freedom to trade and did all they could to prevent these people from attending the sales. A book entitled *Confessions publiques d'un brocanteur* (Public Confessions of an Antique Dealer), published in Amsterdam in 1776, reveals some of the more dubious practices of the time. "Whenever we located some paintings at a public sale which we estimated to be of value, we would group together in pairs, and move over to wherever we saw individual enthusiasts who looked like they might bid for them, where we would keep repeating: "What a pity it's a copy! If only it were an original!" Or sometimes, simply: "It's a daub, what a nasty piece of work." So it was knocked down to my colleagues for next to nothing. (…) We would go to sales at which there would normally be two other groups like ours: we would only bid against each other for the sake of appearances; the paintings were knocked down to us for next to nothing and we would share the spoils by a method which we called 'revision.'" A few years later, Sébastien Mercier tried to put amateurs on their guard against "those who prevent the public from taking advantage of bargains," but Diderot expressed his respect for dealers in paintings, making a point that is applicable to art dealers in general: "They are neither painters, nor sculptors, nor literary figures. They are purely and simply dealers in pictures. However, they are able to judge them better than any painter, writer, or artist; and if the writer shrugs his shoulders at the painter and if the painter laughs it off, the painter shrugs his shoulders at the antique dealer and the writer laughs in turn. Does

the antique dealer have a better innate understanding of drawing, of color, and the magic of light and shade than any of us? Not at all, but he has spent forty years of his life looking, comparing, buying, and selling. His knowledge is the result of his expenditure in time and money." In the last years of the pre-revolutionary period, Paris became the center of the European art market. Objects were sold here which had been brought from the United Provinces, Italy, and Great Britain. Agents came to do deals on behalf of the Tsarina Catherine II of Russia, German sovereigns, and English lords. The sales also became crucial for the reputation and income of the dealers. They attracted a select public of buyers and sellers and mobilized a considerable fortune.

These activities were far removed from those of the simple junk merchants whose more picturesque operations were often the brunt of parodies performed on stage. Here is an extract from a play that was popular at the time:

"Do you have anything in your shop that is attractive, rare, or really curious?" "Yes, sir, I have a great number of such pieces; but the oldest curiosity that I have in my store is a little copper plate which is engraved with the discourse which Adam made to the mother of us all at their first meeting, and the reply of the good Eve. Due to the passage of time, the letters have become illegible, but that is what determines the price."

CABINET BOTTOM
Although the bottom of the cabinet, belonging to a pair, is decorated with marquetry panels by André-Charles Boulle showing mythological figures, it is stamped by the cabinet-maker Joseph Baumhauer, who worked during the second half of the 18th century under the direction of the draper (*marchand mercier*) Julliot. Wallace Collection, London.

LE DÉJEUNER
François Boucher, 1739. Louvre Museum, Paris.

THE TRADE IN CURIOSITIES DURING THE FRENCH REVOLUTION

The turmoil of the French Revolution obviously did not favor the antiques trade. Wealthy art lovers emigrated and those who stayed on but escaped arrest did their best to appear inconspicuous. The auction rooms and antique stores were abandoned by their regular customers. Yet during this period, a large number of great works of art and objects of value came onto the market which for centuries had remained in private collections or the treasure-houses of churches. The property of emigrants was confiscated and became "national property," their collections were sold or sometimes pillaged. Dealers who had plenty of stock would display outstanding items on the Place du Carrousel, but buyers showed an unusual reluctance to come forward. Who would risk his head for the sake of a souvenir of the Ancien Régime?

The sale of the royal furnishings organized in the former apartments of the Princess de Lamballe at the Versailles castle drew an exceptionally large crowd of bidders, consisting mainly of antique dealers and *fripiers* who "being by their situation more able to appreciate the rare items presented for auction, assured themselves

of exorbitant profits" by resorting to underhanded practices, if Abbot Grégoire is to be believed. The dealers were joined by former cabinet-makers to the Crown such as Riesener and Jacob, who wanted to buy back the furniture they had delivered as well as a few drapers-cum-antique dealers. A few nobles even ventured as far as Versailles to try and adorn themselves in the spoils of a discredited regime. The largest purchases were made by a dealer named Rocheux acting on behalf of a wealthy enterprise from Strasbourg, a bookshop run by the brothers Treuttel, themselves associates of the Eberts brothers, respectively a banker and a supplier to the German courts. Their interest in purchasing furniture at Versailles is understandable, especially as payment was to be made in Assignats, the French paper money which was devaluing on a daily basis, and could be exchanged on the other side of the border for more stable currencies. Yet foreign collectors were very rare. Despite a heavy advertising campaign in the press of Holland and Hamburg, few wanted to risk entry into revolutionary France. They preferred to send an agent or place their purchasing instructions with a Parisian dealer who was a member of the drapers' guild, and who himself commissioned *fripiers* and junk merchants. In one year, from August 25, 1793 to August 20, 1794, 17,182 lots of furniture, porcelain, glassware and mirrors, ormolu, and other precious objects from the royal collections fell under the hammer. More often than not, the sales were more of a madhouse lottery than an auction, in which valuable objects were jumbled up indiscriminately with those of lesser interest.

Many great houses and castles were destroyed or despoiled of their furnishings. The Sceaux castle was razed to the ground in 1798 and, at almost the same time, the furnishings of Montreuil, Marly, Rambouillet, Saint-Cloud, Fontainebleau, and Chantilly were auctioned off under disastrous conditions. Many stately homes were also the victims of appalling vandalism due to property speculation or were attacked by the "black gangs" who made a fortune by stripping them and selling off cheaply the paneling, mantelpieces, mirrors, and staircases. The Revolution did not spare the churches and convents of France and there were no scruples about pillaging their treasures. The most precious relics and beautiful religious sculptures were sold at knockdown prices as instruments of superstition by ignorant junk merchants who rid themselves of their spoils without making much profit from them. Englishmen such as William Beckford and Samuel Rush Meyrick, fascinated by the medieval period, were thus able to form their superb art collections during these years of neglect.

UNDER THE DIRECTOIRE

During the first years of the Directoire, Paris seemed to have been transformed into a huge flea market at which impromptu sales were held on every street corner. Parisian antique dealing entered a period of unprecedented commercial activity, a frenzy of buying and selling. The "barterers" (*troqueurs*), as they were known at the time, laid out on the pavements of the wealthy neighborhoods of Paris whatever they had been able to glean from the palaces, mansions and churches. The major items were sold by dealers in luxury goods, whose stores were frequented by members of the new society. An advertisement in the official gazette, *Affiches et Annonces,* for Pluviôse Year II (January, 1794) reads: "Store of Citizeness Mauduit, dealer, sells furniture from Versailles and the Trianon at fixed prices." Specialty shops were located along Left Bank of the Seine. The Collège de France contained a row of such stores where from 1793, one could admire the displays in the windows of Citizenesses Lambertin, Lafaytière, and Dermain, "sellers of paintings, art objects, and curiosities," and visit one of the biggest and most important antique stores of the period, that of Citizen Pierre Duval. Strollers on the lookout for good deals were rare, although a few got caught up in the game. One of them, the Viscount of Ségur, a Field Marshal's son, even opened an elegant store of his own, to sell off the old pieces he had come across during his wanderings throughout the city.

JASPER CASKET MOUNTED BY GOUTHIÈRE
In the 1780's. It was purchased by the Queen Marie-Antoinette at the sale of the Duke of Aumont in 1782, with expert merchant Le Brun as middleman. Wallace Collection, London.

**ENGRAVING DEALER
AT THE ENTRANCE OFFICE
OF THE LOUVRE**
P. A. de Machy, 1791.
Carnavalet Museum, Paris.

At the same time, the auctions started up again. Ever since the privileges of auctioneer-valuers were withdrawn in 1793, any citizen was entitled to usurp the role. An upholsterer named Audry announced the sale in his store of "furniture and effects originating from persons recently sentenced" and the cabinet-maker Foix transformed his workshop in the Rue Saint-Denis into an auction-room to sell "all sorts of curiosities." The homes of emigrants and of those convicted by the tribunals, national repositories, the Paris Office of the National Domain, and the Châtelet, all became impromptu auction-rooms. The Palais-Royal, rebaptized the "Maison-Égalité" and the former *Comédie Italienne,* a theater, were also used as auction rooms, but the largest center of trade in curiosities remained the same as at the end of the Ancien Régime, the Hôtel de Bullion. The same leading players, the merchants Constantin, Clisorius, Lebrun, Paillet, and Regnault, continued to operate there. There was so much merchandise that sale catalogues were no longer being produced.

The terrible financial crisis of 1795 increased the pace. Inflation was so rife that an idea which had been floating around for some time was now applied without hesitation. During the session of the 23rd Brumaire of the Year II (November 13, 1793) a member of the commission of the Provisions proposed: "Let us finance the Republic with foreign trade; we shall assemble English merchandise in good condition, Dresden china, mirrors, chimney ornaments, lace and small valuable furnishings which now grace the houses of emigrants; let us channel them from the various parts of the country to the ports of the Republic (…) Let us set up four dealing houses which have ample lines of credit and which will appear to be operating for their own benefit, but which, in reality, will be trading on behalf of the Republic."

Customers were still few and far between, however, and the smaller dealers generally did not have the necessary capital to allow items to languish in their store for a number of years. Only a few could permit themselves the luxury of building up stock. At the time, the fashion was for strict, uncluttered neoclassicism of which the arbiters were David, Jacob, Percier, and Fontaine. Only the best items of furniture from the Ancien Régime had retained their prestige and members of the Directoire searched the furniture repository at Versailles, Fontainebleau, and Compiègne for items with which to furnish their apartments in the Luxembourg Palace. The confirmed prestige of these old spoils probably also attracted the new rich. One of the known collectors of the period, Dominique

Vivant-Denon, a frequent visitor to the salon of the Empress Josephine, shared the tastes of the antique-lovers of the Ancien Régime. His collection included fragments of ancient architecture, stone carvings, Chinese porcelain, and Italian majolica, and even Boulle furniture and paintings by the Old Masters. But Denon was not merely content with buying: "I am a merchant," he confessed, "and everything I have is available to anyone who wants to give me the wherewithal to buy something more beautiful than what I already possess." His office had become a curiosity shop and was visited like a saleroom or an odds and ends store, even by some foreigners. Princess Lubomirska, a friend of the Polish royal family, found herself in Paris during those crazy years and after protracted negotiations, she would purchase numerous paintings and valuable furniture for the collections of the Counts Potocki. The wealthy Englishman, William Beckford, was just as skillful at acquiring quality pieces for a bargain price and Governor Morris, the U.S. ambassador, acquired a number of royal pieces through middlemen. From someone named Gorey, he bought "two mahogany dressing-tables" for the sum of 900 livres, for which the dealer had paid 141 livres 19 sols at the sales at Versailles. Another purchaser of items from Versailles, Jean-Louis

DOMINIQUE VIVANT-DENON
The *Portrait of Vivant-Denon* amid his collection, after René Berthon. Colored lithograph by Jean-Baptiste Mauzaisse and Caumoin, 1844. Denon Museum, Chalon-sur-Saône.

Collignon, who had been a furniture seller even before the Revolution, stocked his store with "beautiful furniture, chandeliers, and antique vases of green porphyry," as well as with contemporary furniture.

On 28 Messidor Year VI (July 15, 1797), masterpieces of medieval art, declared "useless for art and for teaching," stored in the treasure-houses of the Abbey of Saint-Denis and the Sainte-Chapelle, were shamefully sold on the order of the Ministers of Finance and the Interior at the Anatomy Room in the Louvre. Incredibly, the items included most of the ornamental clasps from the collection of the church of Saint-Denis, including two gold and silver eagles, and the cope-holder of Anne of Brittany. Those objects which were considered to be "useful to art and teaching" were piled into makeshift warehouses before being sent, in principle, to a museum, library, or school. The operative words are "in principle" because the negligence and dishonesty of the agents responsible for supervising these warehouses allowed some of these items to be traded on the international scene.

Alexandre Lenoir, the "general guardian" of items stored at the convent of the Petits-Augustins (which was to become the Museum of French Monuments), was far from being an orthodox curator. Although credit is due to him for saving many medieval masterpieces from destruction, he only vaguely respected the concept of "public domain," selling and exchanging items deposited with the museum in order to buy others which he considered to be worthier of interest. He was in questionable commerce with the biggest stained glass merchant of the period, the German Christopher Hampp, and did not hesitate to organize auctions right inside the Convent of the Petits-Augustins.

FROM PARIS TO LONDON

European collectors were the first to benefit from the bargains that were then to be had on the French market. Parisian merchants had not been able to travel since the outbreak of the revolutionary wars. The exceptions were the Ebert brothers from Strasbourg and a man called Ferrière, who held public auctions of furniture and other royal objects in Hamburg. However, at the time it was mainly the English collectors and dealers who dared to seize the opportunities. Thanks to their spoils from the former French kingdom, they were able to build London into the new capital of the art market. As early as 1790, the British market was flooded with furniture and valuable objects being sold by French aristocrats who had emigrated to London as soon as the first

**CHEST, DECORATED
WITH JAPANESE LACQUER**
Bought by William Beckford
in 1797 at the sale of the
Duke of Bouillon, with Parisian
draper (*marchand mercier*)
Darnault as intermediary.
Victoria and Albert Museum,
London.

signs of unrest erupted in 1789 and had been ruined by the lively and lavish lifestyle on the other side of the Channel. The British were unable to visit France to attend the great auctions of the Revolution, however. Although they travelled as far as Holland and Hamburg to buy royal furniture which was being resold there, they relied mostly on the cunning of French and other foreign agents to acquire items directly in Paris. When the political situation made it impossible for Beckford to cross the Channel or send his English agent, he used the famous Paris *marchand mercier* Darnault, through whom he bought a number of valuable objects at the sale of the collection of the Duke of Bouillon in 1797, such as a particularly beautiful Japanese lacquer chest which had been in the collections of Cardinal Mazarin.

The definite preference of Beckford's contemporaries for the vestiges of French royalty caused them to rush to France during the twelve months of the Peace of Amiens (March 1802 to March 1803). Sir John Dean Paul, a banker and collector, happened to be in Paris at the time and affirmed his pleasure at "being able to purchase certain handsome items of furniture and art objects resulting from the pillage of the various palaces or houses of the nobles during the Terror." He added that "There were also a large selection to be found among the deal-ers but these were not displayed to the public and one had to ask for them specially. In one of these places, having climbed a few stairs and crossed a dirty, paved courtyard, we discovered a warehouse of new and old furniture. The men were filthy and wore no topcoats, like mere laborers, yet they stored their tobacco in magnificent gold boxes." Lord Hertford, Sir Charles Long, and Sir Watham Waller, also in the capital, were shrewd advisors to the Prince of Wales in his acquisitions. The future King George IV, fascinated with France, was such an avid collector that a single invoice often lists several exceptional pieces, as evidenced by the invoice from the merchants Daguerre and Lignereux, dated April 21, 1803, which mentions a pair of candelabra "in the Egyptian style," a cabinet-cum-bureau, two closet bases decorated with panels of Florentine pietra dura "in the antique taste" and an ormolu clock in "in the Apollo style."

THE CONSULATE AND THE EMPIRE

The situation gradually changed under the Consulate and the Empire. Although Napoleon continued to furnish the state apartments of the Tuileries and Saint-Cloud with a few masterpieces from the former royal furniture repository and bought a Boulle chest of drawers in 1805 from Rocheux, 8, Rue de la Concorde, for the palace of Fontainebleau, the Emperor preferred to advocate modern craftsmen and manufacture. "His majesty wants to encourage the making of new things and not buy old ones," was his reply in 1809 to "la femme Aulmont" who offered him a masterpiece by Riesener. Yet the number of listed antique dealers increased. In 1801, there were nine public auction houses run by antique dealers (six of them at the Palais-Royal) and there were 12 "curiosity shops," though the list continued to include "dealers in natural curios."

In addition, some upholsterers and furniture sellers also sell second-hand objects like Collignon. All these were located in the neighborhood of the Palais-Royal and along the Left Bank. In 1810, there were 30 or so sellers of curios, of whom one third were on the Left Bank, on the Quai Voltaire and the Quai Malaquais, in the Rue de Lille, the Rue des Saints-Pères and the Rue de Varenne. The merchants of the Palais-Royal began to migrate to the "Grands Boulevards," while merchandise of average quality could be found with junk merchants, scrap metal dealers, and peddlers who sometimes got their hands on interesting pieces, as well as in private collections. Napoleonic France developed an interest in antique weapons, opening up another outlet on the Paris market. The earliest enthusiasts were French officers whose collections were enriched directly from the arsenals of the conquered armies and who made off with swords, sheaths, trophies and armors without the need for any broker, dealer, or agent. Some of them, such as General Elbe and Baron Percy, created genuine collections, whose various items were carefully chosen for reasons of historical or esthetic value. Very early on, the pragmatist Alexandre Lenoir, former director of the Museum of French Monuments, and a few dealers such as Willemin, sensed how profitable the trade in weaponry would be and decided to take a chance in the market. Their intuition proved correct and brought enviable results because, after 1820, wealthy Britons such as the learned Samuel Rush

ALEXANDRE LENOIR, Curator of the Museum of French Monuments from 1790 to 1816, is shown by the painter Geneviève Boulard as being the main protector of the French patrimony. He rests his hands on his catalogue of the French Monuments. Carnavalet Museum, Paris.

Meyrick and the novelist Sir Walter Scott, scoured the Continent in search of daggers, unusual pistols, arms with secret compartments, habits and armor, in order to transform such British stately homes as Goodrich Court and Abbotsford into medieval domains. After Waterloo, a brisk trade developed across the Channel, one of the main protagonists being Louis Henri, a Paris dealer.

THE RESTORATION OF THE FRENCH MONARCHY

Louis XVIII and Charles X made do with the furniture which had been installed by Napoleon, and those emigrants who now felt it safe to return generally disdained the idea of buying back items that had been confiscated from them. The French fashion no longer favored furniture inlaid with elaborate marquetry and adorned with porcelain plaques. The official furniture repository thus proceeded to sell such items at auctions in 1826 and 1827. British collectors, always in the forefront of fashion, took full advantage of these sales. On the other hand, the appeal of the Middle Ages and the Renaissance grew stronger. The marked interest since the days of the Empire for the medieval scenes described in French as *troubadour* continued with Pierre Revoil, a painter of historic scenes, who bought such artefacts in order to depict them in his paintings and have his students copy them. Some collectors, such as the Countess of Osmond, created Gothic boudoirs, ordering furnishings "in cathedral style" from cabinet-makers. This fashion, also encouraged by the Duchess of Berry, was accompanied by a genuine rediscovery of the Middle Ages. Objects that had been despised for 300 years now suddenly found themselves highly prized by the connoisseurs, who managed to amass a surprising hoard of treasures by taking advantage of the ignorance of the dealers. Alexandre Lenoir was a pioneer of this barely explored wealth of

M. SAUVAGEOT'S APARTMENT
A view of one of the rooms of the apartment of Monsieur Sauvageot, 56, Rue du Faubourg-Poissonnière, before his collection was transferred to the Louvre. Arthur Henri Roberts (1819-1900?). Louvre Museum, Paris.

material. When his Museum of French Monuments was dispersed in 1815, mainly in order to return treasures that had been removed from places of worship in order to save them from destruction, it became an opportunity to place certain pieces on the market, such as the steel chest depicting biblical subjects which had been bought by Lenoir in 1802 "from citizen Scellier, merchant, Rue de Seine," and subsequently acquired by Beckford. Another early collector, Alexandre du Sommerard, had begun his collection under the Empire. In the 1820s, he collected a group of romantic-style pieces for his house on the Rue de Menars, where suits of armor, pottery, enamels, carved ivory, and German stoneware were displayed on Renaissance credenzas.

Toussaint Grille, Pierre Révoil, Edme Durand, Alexandre-Charles Sauvageot, and Dominique Vivant-Denon also formed collections of unprecedented opulence. It was the era when fragments of Gothic architecture and woodwork from churches could be purchased for next to nothing, when stained glass, chalices, and enameled plaques were sold for the price of the raw materials. At Lherie's store, Sauvageot acquired for 200 francs a magnificent bowl from the dinner set supposedly belonging to Henry II, and Vivant-Denon bought a mourner from the tomb of Anne of Burgundy in a Paris junk shop.

A total of 44 antique dealers are listed for 1820 in the *Almanach du Commerce*. One third still operated from the Left Bank and two-thirds from the Right Bank. The migration toward the Grands Boulevards intensified and began a timid advance to western Paris. The Rue Saint-Honoré and the surroundings of the Louvre regained their traditional importance.

Many amateur collectors decided to start trading and proved to be excellent dealers. For example, the knowledgeable Edme Durand, despite his preference for antiquities, became associated at times with dealers such as Rollin, an expert in medals. His method was very simple. He would usually purchase a whole collection, such as Baron

Percy's arms collection, then add to it, and re-auction a few years later. In the 1830s, collectors became more and more numerous, Vivant-Jean Brunet-Denon, the nephew of Dominique Vivant-Denon, as well as Pourtalès, Baron, and Vivenel amongst them. The State finally recognized its role as keeper of the national heritage and began to amass a collection of medieval and Renaissance objects. Edme Durand sold a large part of his treasures to the Louvre in late 1824, and Pierre Revoil's collection was acquired in 1828.

THE JULY MONARCHY—LOUIS-PHILIPPE

Louis-Philippe's accession to the throne in 1830 provided further impetus to the trade in antiques. First of all, the king, who had acquired a taste for decoration with the refurbishment of the Palais-Royal and Neuilly, intended to restore the royal residences and turn Versailles into a historic monument. To accomplish his objective, Louis-Philippe used the resources of the royal furniture repository and especially its "storage room of rejects". Whenever needed, the repository ordered cabinet-makers and craftsmen in metalwork to produce furniture and items in period style or to make reproductions. The king also dealt directly with dealers in curios such as Desperié or Poirier. At the time, concepts of style and authenticity were still relative. The primary consideration was the apparent uniformity of the furnishings, in a desire to evoke a particular period.

The king may have been interested in historic reconstruction but his eldest son, the Duke of Orleans, was "avid for antiques, curios, old pitchers, chinoiserie, wrought iron, and porcelain." He hunted through the furniture repository, decorating his reception room with an eclectic mix which earned it the title of The Antique Room. There were gothic armchairs (in fact "Etruscan-style"), the king's desk made by Oeben and Riesener, corner-pieces by Carlin, and a tall case clock by Riesener. To make it more comfortable, a few rococo armchairs were added.

ALEXANDRE DU SOMMERARD
By Adolph Godard,
circa 1835.
Cluny Museum, Paris.

The duke also visited the antique dealers along the Seine regularly. He bought two small Gothic chairs, a piece of Boulle furniture and a flower-vase in Urbino pottery from Mademoiselle Roussel whose store was on the Quai Malaquais, and two Boulle marquetry clock-cases from Escudier, on the Quai Voltaire. His purchases on the Right Bank were as follows: a bronze mirror frame and a piece of furniture decorated with mosaics of birds and ormolu from the Widow Jamard on the Rue Louis-le-Grand, and Chinese or Japanese porcelain often mounted in gilt bronze from A. Leblanc on the Rue Sainte-Anne. His antique-hunting habits did not prevent the duke from ordering modern furniture in the neo-Louis XIV Boulle style from Alexandre Bellangé for his dining room or to make purchases from designers at "exhibitions of the products of industry." The Duke of Orleans was assisted in his remodeling projects by Eugène Lamy, who thus represented a new type of middleman in the trade in antiques–the interior decorator. On intimate terms with his clients, the interior decorator suggests a decor which suits their collections or advises them to buy items that he knows to be on the market. "For example, I have seen some charming ormolu which the Furniture Repository would gladly purchase and which are real finds."

The furniture of the Ancien Régime was not the only subject of enthusiasm: the love of medieval art continued to assert itself. Du Sommerard left his apartment for the Hôtel de Cluny in the Latin Quarter, where he arranged a series of rooms on historic themes. His love of realism even caused him to place a figure clad in a monk's habit in the chapel. The Du Sommerard Museum could be visited upon purchase of a ticket and reflected the Romantic tastes of the period, fueled by Victor Hugo's novels. *The Hunchback of Notre-Dame* contains descriptions which fired the enthusiasm for the Haute Epoque (from the Middle Ages to the 16th century) where the dark shadows of the medieval period mingle with the Spanish gilding of the Golden Age (16th century). Hugo was aware that whole segments of the national heritage had disappeared and he was one of the first to fight for the preservation of historic monuments. His denunciation of those who were dismantling the castles stone by stone–who were called "the Black Gang" at the time–did not prevent him from purchasing remnants of the fast-disappearing past from their "fences," the second-hand dealers. These included the tapestry panels which he bought from a dealer in the Rue de Lappe, "silent witnesses to the murder of Monaldeschi in the bedroom of Queen Christina of Sweden at Fontainebleau."

It was during this period that Jean-Baptiste Carrand, an archivist from Lyon, came onto the scene. Carrand took up residence in Paris in 1830 and earned a living as an expert and advisor to the collectors Debruge-Duménil, Jules Labarte, and Prince Soltykoff, buying on their behalf and restoring many items with the help of his son, Louis.

The royal family followed the trend. The Duke of Orleans himself revealed "a very modern passion (…) for old furniture, remains, and old relics from centuries past." His sister, Princess Marie, bought out of her own pocket furniture which was partly composed of older elements in order to create a Gothic room in the Tuileries which she used as a studio. She hunted in person for pottery and knicknacks which were crowded onto a dresser.

The novelist Honoré de Balzac, himself a collector, decorator, and specu-lator, discovered in the antique dealer a magician who could open the doors to dreams, longings, and wealth. The seller of curiosities is depicted as the keeper of a treasury and a tempter by Raphaël de Valentin, the desperate hero of *La Peau de Chagrin,* who enters a shop on the Quai Voltaire to forget his misfortunes, and discovers the shagreen talisman which brings him wealth at the cost of his life.

In *Le Cousin Pons,* the collector Pons, an old-fashioned, pathetic misfit but a scholar, hunts avidly for antiques in Paris, haunting the same places as his creator, Balzac, "among the Auvergnats (junk dealers coming from the province Auvergne,) those satellites of the Black Gang who carried in their waggons the wonders of Pompadour's France." Cousin Pons, who had begun antique-hunting in the days of the Empire, avoided the great dealers and believed in "finds." "Yesterday, I was stunned by this divine masterpiece which Louis XV must certainly have commissioned. How did I ever find a fan on the Rue de Lappe! From an Auvergnat, a peddlar who sells bits of copper, scrap metal, gilded furniture?" In his *Iconographie du Genre Brocanteur* (Iconography of the Genus Antique Dealer) Balzac paints the portrait of Remonencq, who successively acts as an agent for curiosity sellers on the Boulevard Beaumarchais and for tinkers on the Rue de Lappe during the French Restoration. He is a scrap dealer in the Marais district, then an antique-hunter in the suburbs for the Parisian merchants. Remonencq still wears the patched velvet coat of the Auvergnat but dreams of wearing one day an elegant top-coat and setting up shop as an expert on the Grands Boulevards. "He wanted to become a wealthy dealer in curiosities, trading directly with collectors." By the end of the novel, Remonencq is the owner of a "magnifi-cent store on the Boulevard de La Madeleine." Balzac's mania for bric-à-brac increased with age and the acqui-sition of an 18th-century mansion to celebrate his marriage to Madame Hanska led him into considerable expenditure. He forced himself to avoid antique dealers. "I would pass antique stores with my head bowed and without going into them," but he sought to justify his passion. "Anyone buying a Boulle bed for less than the cost of a grocer's bed or a mahogany bed is neither a spendthrift nor a maniac for bric-à-brac," he wrote to Madame Hanska. The "Boulle" bed, lavishly decorated with marquetry, was a typical 19th century creation, and might

ESCUDIER
Label of the curio merchant established quai Voltaire. Roxane Dubuisson Coll.

lead one to think that Balzac shared the lack of discernment of his contemporaries when it came to antiques. The interiors described by Balzac are representative of a period when antique furniture and contemporary creations were combined but when rooms were beginning to be decorated in a particular overall style. This was a formula adopted by the banker William Hope in the opulent residence he had built on the Rue Saint-Dominique. The Haute Epoque and the Italian Renaissance each had a place in the anterooms, along with Limoges enamelware and reliefs by Della Robbia. Although the huge dining room was entirely English mahogany, the bedroom was neo-Renaissance. The boudoir was dedicated to the latter reigns of the Ancien Régime, including small items of rosewood furniture decorated with porcelain plaques and rococo chairs. The reception rooms were supposed to evoke the grand apartments of Versailles. In the main sitting room, the fireplace and mantelpiece were designed by the architect in Louis XIV style, with a few modern touches such as the fifteen candelabras and three chandeliers in Japanese porcelain and the ormolu rocaille of the ballroom. The innumerable medieval pieces, carved ivories and Limoges enamel, the 18th-century *objets de vertu,* collections of Renaissance ornamental engravings, enamel miniatures and portraits, Chinese and Japanese lacquer and porcelain, stained glass, triptychs, manuscripts, glassware and antique terra cotta, Egyptian antiquities, an abundance of chalices and objects inlaid with hardstone gems, small Renaissance and 17th-century bronzes, and Renaissance pottery, to say nothing of the "old Sèvres" porcelain, made him a typical collector of his time.

BALZAC, LA PEAU DE CHAGRIN
Raphaël de Valentin and
the curio merchant.
Illustration of 1838.
Balzac Museum, Paris.

The liberties taken with old furniture, which was sometimes "improved," copied, or mixed with furniture "in the style of…" was the work of dealers who often sold antiques alongside contemporary pieces. In their records, some, such as Poirier, Soliliage, Despériés, and Gansberg, call themselves "seller of curios" or "seller of antique furniture," such as Chapsal, or even "seller of art objects and curiosities." Three of the antique dealers frequented by the Duke of Orleans–Mademoiselle Roussel, the Widow Jamard, and Escudier–ceased trading in the middle of the reign, and the catalogues produced for the sale of their stock reveal the diversity and the nature of the "art and luxury objects" they sold. At the top of list there is Boulle marquetry and furniture inlaid with pietra dura–desks, commodes, chests of drawers, tables–furniture of the "Riesener type" with marquetry and rosewood veneers, decorated with plaques of Sèvres porcelain and with bronze–such as that owned by Mr. Hope–as well as carved wooden Gothic furniture in the "Louis XII style"–dressers, credenzas, and sofas–and Renaissance beds "in the style of Jean Goujon." Then come mirrors, long-case clocks, bronzes, little commodes or dressing tables, small medieval objects–diptychs, ivories, stained glass–oriental weapons, dishes by the ceramist Bernard Palissy, and western and oriental china. Certain pieces of furniture, such as the "beautiful mirrored rosewood closet whose curved door is decorated at the top with a lovely turquoise blue Sèvres porcelain plaque," are obviously contemporary creations. Monsieur Escudier also offered additional items that were indispensable for an opulent mansion such as that of the Duke of Orleans who bought Boulle marquetry cases from him for his Antique Room. Certain manufacturers such as the metalworker Feuchères, who added bronze parts to the Widow Jamard's old china, decided to offer their clientele old objects, in addition to the clocks, sconces, and bronze items made by them. In 1826, there were more than 30 sellers of curios, some of whom began to specialize. Brunswick at 50, Rue Croix-des-Petits-Champs, added "curiosities in ancient, antique, and foreign weaponry" after his name. In 1839, there were 65 such merchants, though some were also manufacturers, such as Cuenot, "bronze items and porcelain flowers, in imitation of Old Sèvres and Saxony," or repairers like Jeandon,

THE RED DRAWING ROOM OF THE DUKE OF NEMOURS
Preliminary sketch for the Duke of Nemours' apartment at the Tuileries, circa 1844. Watercolor by Eugène Lamy. Museum of Decorative Arts, Paris.

"antiques dealer, cabinet-maker and marquetry maker, repairer of antique furniture." Warehouses and repositories from which sales were also made began to make their appearance. These included Romagnesi Jeune, "art objects warehouse," and Thedenat Duvent, "artistic agency, placement and sale of art objects and curios exhibited to the public, advances paid on items deposited," at 32, Rue du Colisée. The upholsterer Dorville, whose store was on the Place de La Madeleine, announced a "major warehouse sale of new and second-hand furniture," while Delaloge Aîné, an upholsterer in 1835, became a dealer in curiosities in 1839. Cabinet-makers also sold second-hand furniture alongside the new. Their number included Alexandre Bellangé, who supplied the Duke of Orleans with neo-Boulle furniture. Another dealer worthy of mention is Georges Monbro who began trading in 1801 as a cabinet-maker and repairer of Boulle furniture. From 1832, he is classified as an "antique dealer and cabinet-maker, shop and repairer of old furniture, curios, art objects." With his son, Georges Alphonse, the business became a "special firm for old furnishings, bronzes, porcelain, manufacturing and repairing workshops" in 1841. His business on the Rue Basse-du-Rempart, opposite the Rue de la Paix, from 1841 through 1853 saw the expansion of his antique dealing. Another example is Edouard Kreisser, who set up shop in 1843 on the Rue Neuve-du-Luxembourg, later moving to Boulevard de La Madeleine, and then to 53, Rue Basse-du-Rempart in 1847, before finishing up in the fashionable 8th arrondissement, on Faubourg-Saint-Honoré, in 1862. He had a bronze factory and a cabinet-making workshop where art objects were also restored. He then ran an "art objects and curiosities store, selling furniture, clocks, candelabra, and Sèvres, Chinese, Japanese and Dresden china and ancient weaponry." The opposite also happened, as in the case of Louis Auguste Beurdeley who set up shop as a curiosity seller in the Rue Saint-Honoré in 1818. He moved his family home in 1840 to the Pavillon de Hanovre, then Rue Louis-le-Grand, on the corner of the Boulevard des Italiens. Beurdeley then added a furniture restoration workshop which became the starting point in his career as a cabinet-maker.

At that time, dealers of the Left Bank stuck to the Quai Voltaire and the Quai Malaquais, and the Rue Jacob, Rue Saint-Benoit, and Rue de Seine, while the area around the Palais-Royal became specialized in dealers of small items and coins and metals. Newcomers to the antiques business were attracted to the Chaussée-d'Antin, the Bourse (stock exchange) district, and the Grands Boulevards. The Rue Saint-Honoré, the Rue de la Paix, and the Rue Basse-du-Rempart were all near the Place Vendôme, which was still untouched. But the most pleasant place for a stroll remained banks along the Seine, as Lady Blessington recalls in her memoirs: "I passed, or lost, a major part of the day in visiting the sellers of curiosities on the Quai Voltaire, and left with a lighter

**THE FAMILY OF
THE DUKE OF ORLÉANS**
In their apartment in the
Marsan wing at the Tuileries.
By Prosper Lafaye, 1845.
Museum of Fine Arts, Dijon.

pocketbook than I had had upon entering. It is impossible to resist, or so it seems to me, the exquisite Sèvres porcelain, which the fine ladies under the reign of Louis XIV (sic) used for their bouquets (…) a crystal flask which had belonged to Madame de Sévigné got the better of my judgement."

SECOND EMPIRE — NAPOLEON III

Under the Second Empire, collecting and interior decorating changed little from the previous generation. Napoleon III and the Empress Eugenie showed a certain interest in the royal origins of furniture and in historic artefacts but did not hesitate to alter them to conform with contemporary taste or to set them alongside modern creations purchased at the World Fairs. Louis XV's bureau made by Riesener which had been placed by the Duke of Orléans in the Marsan wing, was moved by the Empress Eugenie to her workroom at Saint-Cloud. She added a corner console by Martin Carlin and the commode belonging to Mesdames at Bellevue, but she modernized some Louis XVI chairs which had belonged to the Count of Artois or Marie-Antoinette by recovering them with button upholstery. She also added two small modern Louis XV tables.

It was on the Empress' initiative that an exhibition was held at the Petit Trianon, in 1867, which was designed to evoke Marie-Antoinette, the "martyred queen," who by then had become a cult figure. The main collectors of 18th-century furniture, such as Lord Hertford and the Baron Double, attended. This first historic recreation was a great success which added more prestige to genuine relics of the Ancien Régime.

This renewed appreciation for the Ancien Régime was picked up by decorators such as Charles Séchan, who began by designing scenery for the Paris Opera, before decorating the modern palaces of the Sultan of Turkey in Istanbul. He commissioned bronzes for his clients but also offered them many antique chairs and items of furniture, serving as an intermediary with dealers. Eugène Lamy continued his career under the Second Empire, acting on behalf of the Rothschilds. James de Rothschild, whose first residence on the Rue Laffite combined neo-Renaissance and modern furniture, was tempted during the July Monarchy of Louis-Philippe by the opulence of the Louis XIV style for his castle in Boulogne. He subsequently commissioned Lamy to decorate the castle of Ferrières which had just been built for him by Joseph Paxton. The watercolors that have survived show that, as in the new mansion of the banker Hope, the tendency to a consistent style persisted as did the liberties taken with antique furniture.

The businesses of cabinet-maker and antique dealer continued to be linked. Kreuft, on the Rue Joubert, sold "old and new luxury furniture," Alphonse Giroux, who had been a manufacturer and cabinet-maker since the Revolution, had a store on the Boulevard des Capucines and was also listed as a dealer in curiosities. When Monbro sold his shop in 1868, the stock of second-hand furniture was almost as large as that of new items, and the furniture was carefully classified as copies, "older copies" or creations, such as the "remarkable piece which won a medal at the exhibition in 1855." Monbro moved to the fashionable 8th arrondissement where he became a "major dealer and expert."

John Bowes, one of his clients, was an Englishman who settled in Paris. In 1852, he married an actress for whom he bought Madame du Barry's former country house at Louveciennes. There, and in their Paris home in the Chaussée-d'Antin quarter, the couple collected 18th-century items to create their Museum of French Art in England. Bowes was not the only Englishman to have adopted an Ancien Régime lifestyle. Richard Seymour Conway, fourth Marquis of Hertford, who had a colossal income of £250,000 a year, bought the castle of Bagatelle and accumulated in his Paris apartment at 2, Rue Laffite, Sèvres porcelain, and 18th-century furniture and objects, but he was more interested in their intrinsic quality than their pedigree, something that was rare for the period: "Less fortunate than some of my fellow *bric-à-brac* collectors, I am unaware of the origins of the items that belong to me. For a long time I have been purchasing here and there anything that I find pretty, most often without the slightest consideration to the usual claims of the merchants. Bronzes, clocks, and furniture, all of it is supposedly made by Riesener or Boulle or Gouthière, and all of it belonged to Marie-Antoinette, Madame du Barry, or Madame de Pompadour." When he liked something, he even had it copied, taking as his example some dealers who specialized in producing molds or casts. He

BAGATELLE,
Under the Second Empire.
Estate of Lord Hertford.
Photograph by Marville.
Carnavalet Museum, Paris.

(following pages)
**VIEW OF THE STUDY
OF THE COUNT OF
NIEUWERKERKE,**
Curator of the imperial
museums of the Louvre.
Charles Giraud, 1859.
Louvre Museum, Paris.

bequeathed part of his collection to his illegitimate son, Richard Wallace, whose taste was more eclectic and covered the Middle Ages and the Renaissance. Wallace then purchased the entire collection of the Count of Niewerkerke. The Count had been an artist, a superintendent of fine art, and a friend of Princess Mathilde, who bought his antique chests from Joyeau or Juste and his furniture from Malinet or Spitzer.

Under the Second Empire, the number of antique dealers increased with the demand. There were 80 of them in 1850, yet 100 more joined their ranks in the fifteen years that followed. Their geographical distribution changed, and many migrated from the Palais-Royal district to the Rue Taitbout, Rue Laffite, Rue Saint-Georges, and Rue de Provence, clustering around the new salerooms on the Rue Drouot which opened in 1851. There was also a move westward to the Place de la Madeleine, a trend which accelerated due to Haussman's

**THE STUDY OF THE EMPRESS
EUGÉNIE AT ST. CLOUD**
Watercolor by Jean-Baptiste
Fortuné de Fournier (1798-1864).
Compiègne castle.

urban development around the Opera. Gleizes is the first to open a shop on the Place Vendôme, at number 3. From the Boulevard des Batignoles to the Place du Château-d'Eau and the Boulevards Richard-Lenoir and Beaumarchais near the Bastille, scrap-merchants and junk-dealers now acquired the status of dealers in curios. The dealers retained a presence on the Left Bank, yet were confronted by the increasing number of booksellers settling on the quays, while the first antique stores opened in the streets of the Faubourg-Saint-Germain in the Rue de l'Université, Rue Saint-Dominique, and even the Avenue de Ségur. Among the specialists, sellers of oriental fabrics and trinkets from China and Japan gained in importance. In 1865, the word "antique dealer" (*antiquaire*) appeared for the first time. It was used by Constantin Schmidt, one of the suppliers to the Count of Niewerkerke: "antique dealer, curiosities, art objects, specialist in cameos and in antique and modern engraved stones for collections and jewelry, 26, Rue Neuve-Saint-Augustin." In 1867, Schmidt was joined by A. Morel, "antique dealer, expert in art objects and curiosities, Rue de Grenelle."

FROM BRIC-À-BRAC TO THE TOWN HOUSE

The late 19th and early 20th centuries saw a swift change in the status of the antique dealer. Edmond de Goncourt notes in his diary for June 17, 1877: "I am astonished to note the revolution that has suddenly occurred among the new generation of *bric-à-brac* sellers. Before, they were dealers in scrap-iron, itinerant hawkers, in a word: peddlers. Today, they are gentlemen in tailor-made suits, purchasers and readers of books, whose wives are as distinguished as any society wife, gentlemen who give dinners where one is waited upon by manservants in white tie and tails. These thoughts struck me as I sampled a birds' nest soup in the home of Auguste Sichel, noticing the equality which the master of the house had now assumed in relation to the wealthy clients who graced his table. Trade—and this trade in particular—no longer puts the seller in a position of inferiority toward the purchaser: on the contrary, the latter seems to feel himself under an obligation to the vendor. Guests included members of the Camondo and Cernuschi families." Times had changed and Goncourt goes on to remember the dealers of his youth: "There were three boulevards, the Boulevard Beaumarchais, the Boulevard des Filles-du-Calvaire, and the

Boulevard du Temple, which were lined from end to end with display windows, and sometimes with outdoor displays, a whole rococo museum. The boulevards also contained straightforward junk shops, dirty stores full of scrap metal, where window-dressing and display, brochures and photographs were still an unknown art. Ignorant of devices and tricks, of how to show a art object backlit, in the half-light of a small improvised drawing room."

The seller of curiosities became an antique dealer and the market acquired an international dimension. Auguste Sichel and Siegfried Bing were great importers of oriental antiquities, and the dealers in 18th century pieces, as Goncourt remarks with distaste, displayed such items in handsome interiors similar to those in their French and American clients' own homes. Frédéric Spitzer, a Viennese living in Paris, opened an antique shop in Aix-la-Chapelle so as to supply his Parisian customers, rich collectors of the Second Empire. Having quickly made a fortune, he settled down in 1878, on Rue Villejust, in the 16th arrondissement, where, having become a collector, he decorated his town house as a veritable museum of decorative arts which he hoped to sell later to the state. "How to contain the shiver of delight at the sight of this fantastic vessel of 17 meters long, 8 meters high, lit by twelve giant stained glass windows, sparkling with iron and guarded by twenty knights in armor," says a visitor. Mounted stones, enamels, ivory, clocks, reliefs, tapestry, dispersed in 1893 in spite of a vague project of the state to buy them, were immortalized in a catalogue which enables us to trace the movements of the items in the great collections of the end of the century. The desire to complete partial series and the dependance on skillful but unscrupulous restorers may have fueled, knowingly or not, a large traffic in fakes.

Another resounding success was that of Jacques Seligman, who had learned his trade at the famous auction house, Hôtel Drouot, before working with the antique dealer and expert Mannheim. In 1880, he opened his own shop on the Rue des Mathurins. "It was a heap of works of art piled one on top of the other," Baron Edmond de Rothschild recounted years later to Germain Seligmann, "But when your father announced a new consignment had arrived, we rushed over there because the best items would go within the hour." Seligman was so successful that in 1900 he could afford premises on the Place Vendôme, a stone's throw from the Ritz, the jewelers, couturiers—and their clients. Seligman's French clients included Édouard André, who with his wife, Nélie Jacquemart, was an avid collector, and the Dutuit brothers from Rouen, who bequeathed their collection to the Petit Palais

RUE LAFFITTE
A drawing room of the town house where part of the Wallace collection was stocked, having been bought in bulk by Jacques Seligman.

museum. He had an auspicious meeting with J. Pierpont Morgan due to the links between the American collector and the fledgling Metropolitan Museum of Art, which subsequently benefitted from his purchases. Jacques Seligman first visited New York in 1905, where he took premises in a huge residence on 36th Street and made an annual presentation of a selection of items from Paris to the greatest American collectors such as Thomas Fortune Ryan, Mortimer Schiff, Henry Walter and Otto H. Kahn. From then on, wealthy Americans would represent the lion's share of his clientele. He could do no less than receive them in just as lavish a style when they visited Paris, so he bought the former residence of the banker Hope on the Rue de Grenelle, which in the meantime had become

known as the Hôtel de Sagan. "Within a few months, the parquet flooring was covered with blue-and-gold Savonnerie carpets and crystal chandeliers hung from the ceiling, with neutral-colored drapes partly hiding the decor." The Place Vendôme premises remained open for passing trade but the regular customers had access to the "Palais Sagan," a perfect setting for the middlemen, the "amateur dealers" who would arrive, as if making a social call, accompanied by their clients. The mansion held special exhibitions which were attended by Paris high society.

Ivories from the Hoentschel Collection were displayed before their departure for New York to Pierpont Morgan (they are now in the Metropolitan Museum of Art). Twenty-nine tapestries belonging to the Sackville family, which came from Knole House and were also bought by Morgan, were shown here, as well as an exhibition of medieval and Renaissance Art held in 1913, under the patronage of the Marquise of Ganay and opened by King Alphonso XIII of Spain. Jacques Seligman's reputation as a magician was confirmed by the purchase of the entire Hertford-Wallace collection of 18th century works of art, which he had acquired sight unseen while they were still

JOHN PIERPONT MORGAN

in bond. The first collector who was admitted to this Ali Baba's cave was Henry C. Frick, who was accompanied by his interior decorator, Elsie de Wolfe. On the following day, the Wallace treasures were on display in the Rue de Grenelle before being sold to the great museums and collectors. Seligman was believed to be capable of anything. When one of his clients, the banker Moïse de Camondo, encountered him at a reception given at the Palace of Versailles in honor of John D. Rockefeller, he hailed him with: "Congratulations, Jacques, I didn't know that you had just bought Versailles!" To which Seligman retorted: "Then you don't realize that I have already resold it!" Seligman became an expert whose advice was sought by politicians in delicate matters such as the German and Austrian reparations and sales by the Soviets in the aftermath of World War I.

Nathan Wildenstein, who was a contemporary of Jacques Seligman, left Alsace in 1870 and opened a modest establishment in the Cité du Retiro in the early 1880s. In 1889, he joined forces with Gimpel to open a gallery in New York where he was represented by his cousin Felix Wildenstein. The clients of Wildenstein & Gimpel included Morgan as well as the currency trader, Julius Blache, and William Randolph Hearst who bought treasures for the castle he had built himself at San Simeon, California. In 1905, Wildenstein bought an 18th-century mansion at 57, Rue de la Boétie, in Paris. "For the family, the financial effort was enormous, but it matched the philosophy of 'onward and upward'. It was a new stage. The stock had to be displayed in the appropriate setting, the 18th century in the service of the 18th century, providing the walls, salons, and galleries. This dramatic backdrop and the atmosphere of luxury were all part of the strategy, but they were also a fantasy," Daniel Wildenstein explained. It was a way of declaring: "We are sick and tired of being treated like shopkeepers." The luxury of the surroundings inspired confidence in some clients, but exasperated others. According to Daniel Wildenstein, his grandmother loved to tell the story of how Mrs. Stern, the banker's wife, said to her: "That's a lovely carpet you have. And to think we're the ones who are paying for it!"

Although antique dealers had branch stores in New York, Paris remained the center of their business activities and they soon realized that finding an outstanding item in Paris itself, or through the intermediary of a Paris dealer in the provinces, endowed the piece with an aura of discovery, as confessed Richard Dreier who once had refused to buy a tapestry of Boucher in New York but did so in Paris some months later at Duveen's for a much higher price: "In Paris you lose your head."

Seligman's competitor and neighbor in Place Vendôme was Joseph Duveen, later Baron Duveen of Millbank, who transformed the family firm Duveen Brothers, founded in 1879, into an international company. Duveen purchased several international collections in their entirety, such as Oskar Hainauer's collection of paintings and antiques in Berlin and Rodolphe Kann's collection in Paris. His American clientele included Benjamin Altmann, Samuel H. Kress, Andrew Mellon, and Joseph E. Widener. Duveen created the *Fragonard Room* for Henry Clay Frick, a decor designed to represent the best in French applied art. He generally spent the winter in New York returning to London in the spring before setting off for Paris, and not returning to London until September. In the courtyard of his Paris headquarters at 20, Place Vendôme, Duveen built a pavilion inspired by Gabriel's Petit Trianon and he remained faithful to the French style for his mansion in New York which he commissioned from the architect René Sergent, specialized in a neo-Gabriel style of architecture. As a Parisian and international celebrity, Duveen became a trustee of many of London's art museums which benefitted from his generosity.

The antique dealer was no longer the doubtful guardian of treasures of whom Balzac had his suspicions, but rather a "weaver of dreams." At least in the eyes of Boni de Castellane, collector and decorator to the core, who had considered founding a "trust of *objets d'art*" with the money of his wife Anna Gould. Thinking about what paradise would be for him, he imagined it as a castle that was constantly being refurnished, of course, and conveniently located near a city whose population consisted entirely of antique dealers. "Among them, I would once again find Seligman, Kraemer, Davies, Duveen, and all those who have given me the greatest satisfaction in my earthly life. Some people have difficulty believing that these men will go to heaven but I have never begrudged them the fortunes that they made at my expense and I am grateful to them for the joy they brought me."

ANTIQUE DEALERS AT THE BEGINNING OF THE TWENTIETH CENTURY

The rise of the top dealers did not diminish the presence of those at the lower end of the market who played the wellknown role of the discoverers. Although the 18th-century masterpieces had long since left the Faubourg Saint-Antoine for the Faubourgs Saint-Honoré and Saint-Germain, new waves of merchandise entered the market. As one of the Goncourt brothers remarked disdainfully: "Crispin, from whom I bought a magnificent bed originating from the castle of Rambouillet and which was allegedly the bed slept in by the Princesse de Lamballe (…) Crispin, whose ground floor premises were once full of flamboyant gilded rocaille, marbles, terra cotta busts, objects of the greatest curiosity, now harbors reproductions of antique furniture, lyre-shaped clocks and sphinx andirons of the First Empire."

In the 1870s, French Empire furniture was completely out of fashion and merely recalled the pomposity of an "official," Napoleonic style. With the birth of the Third Republic, there was a backlash against all imperial styles. Castles, such as that of Compiègne, were emptied of their souvenirs then turned into museums. Malmaison was

**HALL OF
THE CASTLE OF FERRIÈRES**
Watercolor by Eugène Lamy,
circa 1860. Priv. coll.

sold by the Public Trustee, and the National Furniture Repository rid itself of a major part of the neo-classical furniture of the former imperial residences. These sales, as well as those of private members of the imperial family, such as Princess Mathilde, flooded the art market at a time when such items were completely out of fashion. Only a few nostalgic scholars, who were more historian than antique collector, went to seek out these treasures which lay dormant in the back rooms of antique dealers. One such collector was Paul Marmottan, a historian of the French Empire. In the little Empire-style house that he built at the family mansion near the Bois de Boulogne, he harbored armchairs that had been delivered by Jacob to Fontainebleau, Consulate period chairs from the Tuileries Palace which had been brought from Malmaison, the Empress's bed and a chest of drawers that had belonged to the minister Mollien. Marmottan was ahead of his time, however, and only artists like James McNeill Whistler or provocative esthetes such as Robert de Montesquiou could praise the Empire style for reasons which the Goncourt brothers considered decadent. Although André, Édouard, and Nélie, bought a set of the finest Empire furniture in 1892, it never graced their mansion on the Boulevard Haussmann, whose ground floor remained doggedly dedicated to 18th-century French furniture, but was later sent to their property at Chaalis to decorate the magnificent so-called "Eagle Room." It was not until the inter-war period that furniture "decorated with swans like bathtubs," which the Princess des Laumes found so amusing at the beginning of *Remembrance of Things Past,* was rehabilitated under the influence of esthetes such as Charles Swann and the Baron de Charlus. The Duchess of Guermantes forgets her former pretensions: "Let me tell you that I have always adored the Empire style, even when it was not fashionable. I remember that at Guermantes, I was roundly condemned by my mother-in-law because I had all these splendid Empire furnishings which Basin had inherited from the Montesquiou family brought down from the attic and used them to furnish the wing in which I lived."

"The Japanese taste" was the only new style that lovers of 18th-century antiques were willing to embrace, as has just been shown in relation to the Goncourt brothers. Isaac de Camondo is an example of the progressive faction among lovers of the Ancien Régime who were daring enough to buy Impressionist paintings. Isaac's cousin, Moïse, remained faithful to the pre-revolutionary French monarchy, to which he decided to build a monument. In 1910, he demolished the grand family home on the Rue de Monceau, which had been built during the reign of Napoleon III, and ordered his architect, Sergent, to build something in the style of the Petit Trianon in Versailles to house his numerous 18th-century treasures. An account book kept by the collector himself keeps record of his purchases and payments by installments, along with remarks on the origins supplied by the antique dealers from whom he bought: "According to a letter from Lion, the pedestal table opposite has always been in the family of Madame de Champeau, allegedly a gift of he Marquise de Pompadour." Although Moïse de Camondo sometimes bought in the salerooms, as did Isaac at the sale of the effects of Baron Double and of Jacques Doucet, he generally made his purchases through dealers, usually Jacques Seligman or his cousin Arnold. Arnold Seligman managed to find the second half of a pair of Garnier side-tables by finding its twin thirty years later at Davis' in London. In addition to the Seligmans, the names of Bensimon, Wildenstein, Barriol, Stettiner, Fabre, Lévy, Eugène Kraemer, Larcade and Guiraud feature in Camondo's notebooks.

The couturier Jacques Doucet had been one of the last great collectors of 18th-century antiques, but he later changed sides and inaugurated the lineage of patrons of modern fine and decorative art. Like Camondo, in 1907 Doucet built himself a neo-Louis XVI mansion on the Rue Spontini, to house the major collections he had been amassing since the 1890s. These were exhibited in a series of display rooms—salons, galleries and boudoirs—which were open to visitors "of quality" every Sunday morning. Was Doucet disappointed in his hopes of attracting members of society who at the time rejected him as a mere supplier albeit one who furnished luxury items? At any event, he decided to sell everything in 1912 and, to general astonishment, announced that at the age of sixty, he

JOSEPH DUVEEN,
With wife and daughter in London.

was going to start collecting contemporary art. This abrupt change of heart was considered by his fellow collectors of 18th-century antiques as a betrayal. While Seligman, Wildenstein, Stettiner, Duveen and the collectors Moïse de Camondo and Henri de Rothschild were fighting over the finest specimens in his collection, Doucet now turned to Paul Iribe, Pierre Legrain, Joseph Csaky, Paul Poiret, Eileen Gray and Jean-Charles Moreux. His new apartments on the Avenue du Bois and in Neuilly now displayed works by Ernst, Picabia, and Duchamp alongside Picasso's *Demoiselles d'Avignon* which replaced paintings by Boucher and Fragonard, and Brancusi ousted Clodion. Only a few Chinese bronzes, some Greek idols from the Cyclades and African masks were retained to vie for attention with contemporary works of art. This early attachment to primitive art, launched before him by the Stoclets in their Brussels palace, was an up and coming trend which was to become all the rage. Fifty years later, Doucet's treasures had themselves attained the status of antiques, and the sale of his modern art collection in 1972 marked the beginning of the fashion for Art Deco among Parisian antique dealers.

From 1900 to 1914, dealers preferred to refer to themselves as "antique dealers" rather than "dealers in curios" although both occupations flourished in the directories. On the eve of World War I Paris boasted around 500 antique dealers and 200 dealers in curios. Some of these also offered an antique restoration service; specialities were confined to arms and armor, jewelry, coins and medals, fans, and lace. Most were concentrated in the 9th arrondissement though the main street of that neighborhood, the Chaussée d'Antin was losing out to the Faubourg Saint-Honoré and the area around the fashionable Parc Monceau (Avenue de Villiers, Avenue de Wagram, Boulevard Malesherbes, Boulevard Haussmann, Rue de Courcelles, Rue de Rome, Rue du Rocher, Rue de Saint-Petersbourg). Some dealers were located in the area north of this 9th arrondissement, spilling over from the Boulevard des Batignolles to the adjoining Boulevard de Clichy. Dealers were beginning to be able to afford

TOWN HOUSE OF JACQUES DOUCET
Hall of the town house of Jacques Doucet, Rue Spontini. Watercolor by Adrien Karbowsky, circa 1905. Library of Art and Archeology Jacques Doucet, Paris.

the most fashionable neighborhood, the 16th arrondissement, and a new concentration emerged on the Left Bank, around Odéon (Rue de Vaugirard, Rue de Tournon, Rue de Férou) and Montparnasse (Rue de Rennes, Rue du Cherche-Midi). Within ten years, the Rue des Saints-Pères and the Faubourg Saint-Honoré contained the highest concentration of antique dealers, while the 8th arrondissement (between the Rue du Faubourg Saint-Honoré and the Rue Saint-Augustin) and the Parc Monceau area experienced significant growth. The same was true of the 6th and 7th arrondissements on the Left Bank. The Champs-Élysées, Avenue Montaigne, and even the Rue de la Pompe became favorite locations on the Right Bank; those of the Left Bank included Place du Palais-Bourbon, Boulevard Raspail and Boulevard Saint-Germain. The map of antique dealer locations would change little until the 1950s.

If the emergence of Art Nouveau did little to affect the parallel development shown hitherto between contemporary creativity and a love of antiques, the relationship became more subtle. In the 19th century, furniture-makers reproduced former styles as they came back in fashion. From 1900, the most sought after antiques were those in the main styles which had inspired the "moderns," so it was contemporary art that set the fashion among collectors. Art Nouveau, for example, was clearly inspired by French rocaille, and its emergence was accompanied by a craze for Louis XV and French Regency styles. In 1905-1910, the creation with Poiret, Iribe and Follot became less flamboyant and there was a return to enthusiasm for the Louis XVI style, and even, just before the outbreak of World War I, a fashion for the Directoire and Consulate periods, hitherto decried for being uncreative, as can be seen in the illustrations in the *Gazette du Bon Ton*. The triumph of Art Deco confirms this trend. Certain designers such as Süe and Mare openly advocated the Restoration and Louis-Philippe as the "last honest styles" in the French tradition, which hitherto had been considered the epitome of bourgeois bad taste. The neo-classicism of the 1920s and the "return to order" in painting even led certain dealers in modern art like Léonce Rosenberg to hang works such as Giorgio di Chirico's *Bathers* and paintings by Severini over mahogany and gilt French Empire commodes, or to display canvases by Picabia in a Louis-Philippe setting.

THE THIRTIES

The advent of the 1930s heralded a new development. The first wave of modernism in architecture and decoration represented by Robert Mallet-Stevens, Le Corbusier, and Pierre Barbe lost its appeal. The economic crisis shook the faith of collectors in a costly and frigid modernity which was not very gratifying. The twin urges of escapism to another era and to a fantasy world caused decorators such as Jean-Charles Moreux, Serge Roche, and Emilio Terry to resort to the baroque and the rocaille, using lighting that tended toward the surrealist. This was a movement that encouraged chance juxtapositions and combinations of styles, giving a certain piquancy to what had only yesterday been considered the height of bad taste, such as mixing Venetian rococo with Napoleon III. Jean-Michel Frank, André Arbus, Louis Süe, André Belloborodof and Emilio Terry incorporated neo-classicism into modernity.

Decoration and interior design were encouraged by the specialist press. Periodicals such as *Vogue, Art et Industrie, Art et Décoration,* and later *Plaisir de France* were dedicated to decoration and fostered creativity and encouraged audacity of all types. Charles de Beistegui, whose apartment had been designed by Le Corbusier, incorporated tufting, Venetian wall sconces, and Baroque blackamoors onto the walls. Coco Chanel had an Empire-style apartment in the Faubourg Saint-Honoré, in which she placed a rocaille sofa in front of a Coromandel screen. Her rival, Misia Sert, made abundant use of mother-of-pearl and the curvaceous shapes of French Restoration furniture. However, the impact of modernity was far from being erased. The dictum of "opulent furniture of the Boulle type in a strictly modernist setting," which was so successful in the 1970s with Charles Sévigny and Hubert de Givenchy, was originally started by Jean-Michel Frank, Eugénia Errazuriz, and Étienne de Beaumont. Eclecticism now became the prerogative of collectors and lovers of antiques.

The increasing role of the decorator and the individualism of the collector changed the role of the antique dealer who had hitherto merely been a supplier of furniture but was now required to help fulfil the fantasies and dreams of his customers. The concepts of purity and consistency of style and collection disappeared in favor of a more creative concept of decoration in which objects were collected less for their intrinsic value than for the way in which they blended into the general theme. Princess of Faucigny Lucinge, writing in *Vogue* of August 1928 about the Paris apartment of her mother-

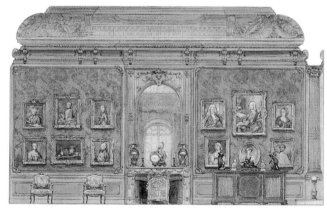

TOWN HOUSE OF JACQUES DOUCET
Main drawing room in the town house of Jacques Doucet, Rue Spontini. Watercolor by Adrien Karbowsky, circa 1905. Library of Art and Archeology Jacques Doucet, Paris.

in-law, Baroness of Erlanger, a great client of antique dealers and secondhand stores, described the new taste. A Baccarat crystal table displayed "a collection of model ships, shells and other objects in glass which gave the impression of an ideal, of something ephemeral, infinitely delicate and dreamlike." Although the collector was aware of the intrinsic value of the objects in her collection, she was more concerned with what could be created through their "confrontation." "She would not hesitate to place a gaudy fairing on a very valuable pedestal table (…) She also loves imitation, and even the parody of an object: blown glass instead of silver ornaments, artificial flowers, fake tapestries. And in furniture, she loves objects made of contradictory materials, such as mirror tables, figurines of shells, glass pipes and pasteboard ships." She considers the antithesis of her taste to be "sterile

APARTMENT OF JACQUES DOUCET IN NEUILLY

Above: The oriental exhibition-room next to the study. Table with lotus by Eileen Gray, glass cases by Marcel Coard, parquet floor and fire-place carpet by Legrain, paintings by Chirico, Mirò and Ernst.

Opposite: The hall. Stool by Jean-Charles Moreux, watercolor by Picabia, painting by Mirò, carpet by Jean Lurçat, green lacquered cupboard with silver disks by Pierre Legrain.

Photographs published in *L'Illustration,* 1930.

reconstructions of the past." As for exotica, Polynesia, which had become a favorite with the Surrealists, was competing with the African art of the Cubists.

This rediscovery of the 19th century and new attitudes to antiques reduced the gap between the antique and the *bric-à-brac* trade. The antique dealers soon embraced the trend and from their colleagues or in the Drouot sale-rooms, they unearthed opaline glass, pale wooden furniture or items adorned with mother-of-pearl which had hitherto been despised. The first directory of dealers, the *Annuaire de l'antiquaire et de l'amateur d'art* published in 1921 by Pierre Dupon lists dealers by specialty. The specialist press echoed new tendencies in articles about dealers who would describe their choice pieces, and fashionable items were soon found in stores which now opened in the most expensive neighborhoods. In February 1939, *Vogue* assured its readers that "the era of empty rooms devoid of objects or trinkets has passed and the hunt for objects, a contagious disease, is now spreading." This is shown by the Louis XV terra cotta of a dog found by Christian Bérard, the Géricault discovered in a junk shop by Boris Kochno, the Renaissance-mounted shell belonging to Arturo Lopez, and the ormolu fish belonging to Mona Williams. The Marquise de Pomereu contented herself with bringing down a mounted porcelain item by Gouthière which had been consigned to the attic.

At the instigation of several antique dealers-decorators such as Serge Roche, the diversification of a wildly increasing market let to the creation in 1932 of an antique art exhibition which was held as part of the *Salon des Arts Ménagers,* a home exhibition which was the forerunner of the current biennial antique fairs. "This is not a selection of rare items, of objects of great value; it is a case of showing the public how an interior can be decorated today, using elements taken from the rich artistic heritage bequeathed to us from the past, by combining woodwork and drapes, furniture and seating, etc." An initial *Exhibition of the art of the table* made it possible to display dining room interiors. In 1934, there was a special exhibition, in which the most prestigious dealers, such as Seligman and Kraemer, participated. Jacques Helft presented a reconstruction of an antique dealer's store circa 1870, Jansen displayed French Regency bookcases, Madame Roy showed a Napoleon III boudoir, Serge Roche a Louis XV palm grove, Férasse a Louis XVI drawing room, and Perret-Vibert a smoking room decorated with Chinese ornaments. From 1936 onward, the theme of "reconciliation of styles" became the norm. Samy Chalom, Serge Roche, and Ramsay tended to concentrate on the 18th century, while Roger Imbert and Jean Chelo preferred the Charles X period (1824-1830).

The era of the great reconstructions in the style of Camondo was perpetuated through newcomers such as François Coty. The perfumer commissioned Seligman to furnish the country house of the Countess du Barry in Louveciennes which he had acquired. The oil magnate Calouste Gulbenkian had a mansion on the Avenue d'Iéna where he had amassed 18th-century masterpieces, but he is also one of the first collectors of Art Nouveau and his immense resources as an international businessman enabled him to bypass the dealers in his purchases from great collectors and even countries, such as Soviet Russia.

In the 1930s, leading firms such as Wildenstein and Seligman launched into the modern art market. Germain, one of Jacques Seligman's sons, bought the *Demoiselles d'Avignon* upon the death of Doucet, and took an interest in Bonnard. In 1925, he held a private showing of French decorative art in his New York residence, including pieces by Ruhlmann, Legrain, Puiforcat, Dunand, Marinot, and Lalique. He subsequently held exhibitions of Picasso's work. In 1938, Georges Wildenstein held a Surrealist exhibition at his *Galerie des Beaux-Arts* on the Faubourg Saint-Honoré, adjoining the family home in the Rue de La Boétie. Wildenstein's scholarly works and the various publications he bought out, such as the *Gazette des Beaux-Arts,* which he created such as *Beaux-Arts Magazine* or which he supported financially, such as Georges Bataille's *Documents,* made him a recognized intellectual as well as a patron of the arts.

HÔTEL DE CAMONDO
The main drawing room
of the town house of
Count Moïse de Camondo,
Rue de Monceau, 1914,
in Paris, currently the
Nissim de Camondo Museum.
White and gold paneling,
1775-1780. Chairs by Jacob,
covered with Aubusson tapestries.

World War II and the German occupation was a disaster for the antiques trade. There were sequestrations, confiscations, and "aryanisations" of property belonging to the Jewish community which affected a large number of businesses and private collectors, whose objects were lusted after by the occupying forces, starting with Goering and Hitler. Forced sales, looting, and hurried transactions prior to flight placed a huge amount of valuable items on the market, encouraging barter, in those dark days of the black market and currency restrictions. These unpleasant and hasty deals attracted a new sort of seedy intermediary, of the type vividly described in the novels of Maurice Sachs. Well-established antique dealers had the choice between closing down or trying to survive. The Germans who seemed to have a predilection for French interiors and especially for large Gobelins tapestries, did business with the firm of Jansen. But this was no time for elaborate receptions or competetiveness in decoration. The collector learned to be discreet.

AFTER THE WAR

After the War, there was a new surge in the market, as if people wanted to forget what had just happened and cling to the extravagances of a distant past that they feared to be gone forever. Some brilliant enthusiasts of Latin-American origin, such as Arturo Lopez Wilshaw, revived the excesses of Louis XIV style. In the same vein, Anténor Patino and his sisters let themselves be guided by Marcel Bisset, an antique dealer who operated from a mansion on the Champs-de-Mars. Charles de Beistegui adapted 17th-century Dutch and Venetian furniture, with interior design by Abraham Bosse and Charles IV in his castle of Groussay, to which Emilio Terry had built an addition in Louis XVII style. This was also the age of the Greek shipping magnate. Emilio Terry was once again at the forefront, recreating the sumptuousness of the Ancien Régime for Stavros Niarchos at the Hôtel de Chanaleilles; Aristotle Onassis bought a home on the Avenue Foch. The French, however, in the person of René Grog, husband of Madame Carven, continued the tradition of an enlightened 18th century. The exhibition entitled *Le Cabinet de l'Amateur* held in the Orangerie in 1956, which devoted a small room to Renaissance jewelry, reinforced the tendency, and antique dealers who had good relations with the Decorative

Arts Museum were invited to exhibit there.

The top decorators of the day, such as Henri Samuel, who restored Guy de Rothschild's Château de Ferrière to Napoleon III style, or Georges Geffroy and Victor Grandpierre, who used a more neo-classical style, became indispensable intermediaries for antique dealers. The work they did was regularly published in magazines. The Parisian market was coupled with a social backdrop in which decor became ever more opulent and ingenious. The links between decoration and antiques, which existed since the beginning of the century, became stronger in large firms such as Jansen, Ramsay or Barroux who dealt in wood paneling as well as old furniture or modern "creation" which were in tune with contemporary needs, such as electrified lamps, coffee-tables and couches.

Two dealers were outstanding purveyors of high 18th-century style: René Weiller, a shrewd, fast-moving businessman, had antique-hunters who now number among the leading antique dealers; and Etienne Levy, whose apartment on the second floor of his gallery on the Faubourg Saint-Honoré paid homage to that exquisite 18th-century decor praised by the Goncourt brothers. Jacques Bonjean, who formerly proned the neo-romantics, continued to favor high Louis XIV that he had launched on the eve of World War II. Mademoiselle Doucet bought the contents of whole castles to restock the large building she occupied on the Place Beauvau, where newly-weds came to look for furnishings as if it were a department store. As for curios, Nicolas Landau, with his aphorisms and culture, and Michel Meyer Sr., with his flair and genius, were the outstanding figures in the trade. On the Rue Amélie, Jacques Kugel was amassing treasures displayed on the Rue Saint-Honoré, where he opened a store in 1970, at a time when the leading players of today were doing their first deals.

New trends began to emerge with the fashion for English furniture launched by Madeleine Castaing, who was thirty years ahead of her time in discovering "amusing" European neo-classicism, in the shape of German Biedermeier, Russian and Nordic pieces which she exhibited at the corner of the Rue Bonaparte and Rue Jacob and in the fresh and casual decors she created for her clients. Jean-Pierre Hagnauer's work was in the same severe yet sumptuous vein. The *Haute Epoque* experienced a revival thanks to its temporary alliance with modern painting and African art, a combination introduced before World War II by such pioneers as Helena Rubinstein and

JEAN-MICHEL FRANK
Drawing room for the
Viscount Charles de Noailles,
Hôtel Bischofsheim,
Place des Etats-Unis,
Paris, circa 1930.
Photo by Man Ray.

**APARTMENT OF
CHARLES DE BEISTEGUI**
Terrace and drawing room of the
duplex apartment created by Le
Corbusier in Paris on a roof of the
Champs-Elysées and decorated by
Charles de Bestegui, circa 1932.

Paul Guillaume and revived again in the 1970s during the second wave of industrial design.

The Retrospective section of the *Salon des Arts Ménagers* expanded. A stroll through the "Rue des Antiquaires" of 1954, with its shops made of "stone facing" or "marble," its public squares decorated with statues and basins, showed decorative art "attempting to illustrate the place of antique furniture and objects in modern life." Some exhibitors, such as Lefebvre-Vilardebo, chose to present their furniture and objects in an "authentically modern" decor. Sometimes, this modern decor was summarized in a few elements, such as pale-colored walls and dark brown carpets (as in the case of Salva), but most used wood paneling as did Samy Chalom (Louis XV woodwork), Ramsay (a Louis XVI drawing room with pale green colored paneling) or Mercier (a small Louis XVI dining room). Barroux reproduced a Louis XIV boutique, Jansen exhibited woodwork of the Directory period from a café in the Palais-Royal, Willy Rémon evoked the marble cladding of Versailles, Carlhian displayed mahogany furniture in front of a panorama by Dufour, while Madame Grandjean (at Jacmar) was inspired by the library at Malmaison. All the French styles were represented, from the Fontainebleau School to the French Restoration, though Sheridan presented "English furniture in a French setting," while Roche and Rotil flirted with Italy and Russia. Specialists in objects (Vandermersch and Nicolier's porcelain, clocks at Diette, ormolu at Baguès, old books at Pierre Bérès) simply produced window displays. Maurice Chalom used a few stone masks to remind everyone that his store was located in Place Vendôme.

In 1956, the Grand Palais became too small for the huge fairs, which had to be moved to new exhibition halls on the outskirts of Paris at the Porte de Versailles. Antique dealers followed the trend by holding a Fair of the Antique Dealers of France, but the name was too clumsy, and the proximity to washing-machines, plus the re-moteness of this neighborhood from the center, was deemed unsuitable. Thanks to André Malraux, French antique dealers and decorators returned in force to the Grand Palais to hold an international, biennial exhibition, the Biennale. The first show was held in 1962, in the form of decorated pavillions. Madeleine Castaing's took the form of a huge rotunda adorned with trellisses entwined with vines and climbing plants. Alavoine presented a roofless folly, Roche and Rotil displayed a *trompe-l'œil* nymphs' grotto, Hagnauer a Chinese pagoda, while Jansen reproduced an arcade of the Palais-Royal. The Biennale became a magnificent event and opened its doors to dealers in "impressionnist and modern" painting, then to the great jewelers. Sometimes a central theme was chosen, as in 1966 when it highlighted the work of Claude-Nicolas Ledoux. A few antique dealers became writers. Some of them, such as Serge Roche and Jacques Helft, did so to make their specialities (mirrors and silverware) better known and understood, others wrote their memoirs. These include Jacques Helft again with his *Vive la chine* (Long Live Antique-Hunting); Yvonne de Brémond d'Ars, who keeps her readers in suspense and like a latterday Alice, invites them to a Wonderland through, "a window open on a corner of the past." As a mark of the growing importance of the profession, an annual guide to antique and curiosity dealers, which became known as the *Guide Emer,* was founded in 1948.

In the mid 1960s, after a cautious flirtation with Danish furniture, there was a return to the tubular modernism of the 1930s, accompanied by a re-issue of the great modern classics, produced by Italian and Scandinavian firms. Beds became lower, floors were lowered to include steps down into a "conversation pit," fitted carpet, mirrors, and gloss paint created homogenous and abstract spaces in which a few old masterpieces floated in brilliant solitude. This union of the old and the new, which had had its beginnings in the 1930s with Nasenta, Jansen or Frank was relaunched by Yves Vidal, who matched the Knoll tuliptable to Louis XV chairs, and Charles Sévigny, who installed Hubert de Givenchy's Boulle closet on smoked glass mirrors. In the same vein, François Catroux hung a "rhinoceros clock" on a brushed aluminum partition wall and Henri Samuel installed works by Balthus over chests of drawers by César, an artist whose furniture designs Jean-Marie Rossi wanted to reproduce. Alain Demachy combined his love of antique objects with that of pure, refined architecture. Modern decor also made it possible to revive the fashion for cabinets of curiosities, as can be seen in the work of the decorators Ortiz-Cabrera or Pierre Delbée's work for Jansen. The cabinets in pietra dura on a plexiglass base were a must which became the speciality of Jean Gismondi. "Paltry Louis XVI" and "18th-century with paneling" styles suffered from this objective alliance between the large and the pure, the rich and the strict. It was an alliance which the "eye" of Andrée Putman regularly featured in the magazine *L'Œil* while Éveline Schlumberger and Axelle de Broglie in *Connaissance des arts* taught their readership how to be "resolutely modern," while remaining "attached to the past." But the person who gave to the world of antiques and decoration its credentials and its poetry was Philippe Jullian, one of the inventors of Art Nouveau, whose *Mémoires of a Bergère* or *La Brocante* can be compared to the reflections of Edgar Allan Poe or Mario Praz on "the philosophy of furnishing."

THE SECOND HALF OF THE TWENTIETH CENTURY

This is where Art Nouveau, followed by Art Deco, made their appearance, one in the mid-50s, the other ten years later. Art Nouveau, launched by inquiring minds such as that of Maurice Rheims and Philippe Jullian, was only briefly in fashion, like the interest in symbolist painting. Although *pâte de verre* and ceramics continued to enjoy a vogue which showed no signs of weakening, furniture however, such as the entire room by Majorelle found by Maria de Beyrie, turned out to be difficult to live with. You had to live in Brussels like Mrs. Gillian Crowett to create a complete French Art Nouveau decor against a background harmony of mauve and green. Art Deco, on the other hand, married perfectly with modern design and its lacquerwork blends with tubes and neon as shown by Andrée Putman. Jean Dunand and Jacques-Émile Ruhlmann became popular with collectors in the world of fashion and showbusiness, creating the era of retro disco. The discreet Serge Royaux was more bourgeois, one of the first to combine Louis XVI and Art Deco, mahogany and Macassar ebony which he found on the Rue Jacob at Jacques Lejeune (*Comoglio*). Leaving the *Marché aux Puces* for Saint-Germain-des-Prés, Art Deco and Art

Nouveau were to be found on the Rue Guénégaud at Stéphane Deschamps and Jacques Denoël, on the Rue Bonaparte at Yvette Barran or later at Félix Marcilhac, ot the Quai Malaquais at Anne-Sophie Duval, while the new generation, Bob and Cheska Vallois, Maria de Beyrie and Philippe Jean were just getting started in the area recently vacated by Les Halles, the wholesale market. Yves Plantin and Alain Blondel in their *Galerie du Luxembourg* showroom offered a brilliant succession of exhibitions and catalogues which paved the way for the rediscovery of Guimard, Dunand, Goulden.

The sale of Jacques Doucet's Art Deco collection in 1972 seriously increased the prices in this emerging market. Pierre Legrain, Marcel Coard, and Eileen Gray were discovered, while the purists went for tubular incunabula and especially the work of Pierre Chareau, who was then at the height of his fame because he combined the innovation of the architect with the craftsman's love of a job well done. The clients for this new market came mainly from the world of fashion, a spiritual bequest from Jacques Doucet. They included Yves Saint Laurent and Pierre Bergé, Karl Lagerfeld, artists such as Andy Warhol, a few enthusiasts such as Hélène Rochas and Kim d'Estainville, and decorators of the new generation such as Jacques Grange who served his apprenticeship at Henri Samuel. The German and American museums did their shopping by snatching prizes from under the noses of the French institutions.

The Post-modernism of the 1980s had a ricochet effect on the world of antiques. Twenty years after Madeleine Castaing and Jean-Pierre Hagnauer had discovered it, the fashion became generalized for a lighter neo-classicism –more playful and eye-catching–a likeable European style as depicted in *La Marquise d'O* by Eric Rohmer. Biedermeier, Gustavian and Russian furniture were sought out in their country of origin and imported by Ariane Dandois or Alain Demachy. Since 1968, Jacques La Querrière had displayed on the Rue de Beaune objects of the *Grand Tour* (trip made by young people from well-to-do families to visit the cultural sights of Europe). In 1976, he launched at the Thenadey Gallery, the overstuffed button upholstery, followed by the decorators Jean-Paul Faye, François Catroux, Alberto Pinto, and Jean-Louis Riccardi. The industrial design of the 1970s seemed tired and boring to fans of Visconti who launched into grandiose recreations of the Second Empire as in his film *Le Guépard*. The 19th century made a strong comeback and Jean-Marie Rossi at *Aveline* unearthed stylistic monstrosities which were the pride and joy of the World Fairs. Together with Albert Bénamou, they hunted for end-of-the-century sculptures and paintings in the vein of Jean-Léon Gérôme, which were considered "pompous." Alain Lesieutre, who was also a great amateur of sculptures and bronzes, bought together symbolists and orientalist artists with Art Nouveau and Art Deco items and furniture in his shops on Rue de Tournon, then Rue de Beaune. Art Nouveau and Art Deco in all their variety took on a European magnitude–from Glasgow to Vienna *via* Darmstadt, Stockholm and Budapest and Moscow–and people like Maria de Beyrie, Antoine Broccardo, Patrick Serraire, Anne-Sophie Duval, Rodolphe Perpitch and Annie Partouche, banished preconceived notions on dates and styles. Several decorators got the message, like François-Joseph Graf.

Éric Philippe, in the Passage Véro-Dodat, lured his clientele into Nordic flights of fancy, through Danish neo-classicism, Swedish grace, and even the latter years of the Wiener Werkstätte. He was the first to present Jean-Michel Frank, whose role as an inspired go-between mediating between men of the world and the world of art symbolized the pre-war period, now as emotionally distant as the Ancien Régime. His crowning achievement, his cult place, the white drawing room designed for Charles and Marie-Laure de Noailles in their home on Place des États-Unis took the place in the nostalgic imagination of Marie-Antoinette's lounging sofa in Versailles. His team included Bérard, Dali, Terry and the two Giacometti, conferring upon him the aura of a guru serving the privileged few. Austere but luxurious, a reinvention of styles, the work of Jean-Michel Frank made it possible to escape the dilemma between old and new in decoration, where color was often eliminated in favor of a drab beige.

ANDRÉ BRETON
AT THE ST. OUEN
FLEA MARKET
Photograph by Gisèle Freund.

The appreciation of Frank spread to Saint-Germain-des-Prés where the Galerie Vallois, Maria de Beyrie, Marc Lamouric, Christian Boutonnet, and Rafael Ortiz joined the pioneers.

At the same time, products of the 1940s were beginning to find their way into the flea market where Yves Gastou, Olivier Watelet, Jacques Lacoste, Aline Chastel, Laurent Maréchal, Christian Sapet, Alexandre Biaggi and Pierre Passebon were reviving the fame of Arbus, Adnet, Dupré-Lafon and Roche. Some avant-gardists such as Allan on the Rue de Lille and Jeanne Gambert de Loche at Jansen on the Rue Royale, were relaunching Jean Royère and Serge Mouille whose whimsical items legitimized and inspired modern designers such as Garouste and Bonetti.

Meanwhile, the museums continued to make purchases from dealers in "high 18th century," such as Didier Aaron, Jean-Marie Rossi, Maurice Segoura, Bernard Steinitz, Jean-Paul Fabre, Michel Meyer, and Jacques Perrin. The Getty Museum, in the person of its curator, Gillian Wilson, dictated his own rules on the market in 18th-century antiques. His main rival was Jane Wrightsmann, collector and patron of the arts who donated most of her finds to the Metropolitan Museum, which were then arranged in period room settings by her friend Henri Samuel. For the Louvre and Versailles the competition was tough, but the dealers bestowed generous deals on the French institutions in proportion to their export turnover. In France, 18th-century antiques continued to do well. Akram Ojjeh and certain other Lebanese middlemen took over, with greater discretion, from the South Americans. Hubert de Givenchy began to abandon the "modernist-Louis XIV" esthetic and recreated a "Boulle-*fermier général*" decor in the various mansions he occupied successively on the Left Bank. Karl Lagerfeld, who abandoned Art Deco in 1975, also re-adopted 18th-century style in his house on the Rue de l'Université.

The 1990s had visibly had enough. Tired of such an amount of originality, there was a frantic escape to the discarded, used and outdated. This was the era of "shabby chic," fostered by *Interior's* and adopted by young households at a loss for ideas. Following this paupers' purge, a desire for structure came to the fore, a desire to return to minimalism into which a few choice items of junk could be incorporated, such as pieces from the 1950s to 1970s, whose wood and iron, corrugated iron and formica, steel and chrome, mirrors and stucco, took on a dignity worthy of the survivors of a century on the turn. At the new *Pavillon des Antiquaires* on the Quai Branly, all the currents of the 20th century–Jean-Michel Frank and Pierre Chareau, Serge Roche and Paul Dupré-Lafon, André Arbus and Jean Royère, returned with the same indulgence. The Art Deco market attempted to revive a few of the great names of the 1940s–which hitherto had been the preserve of promoters–like Marc du Plantier or Paul Dupré-Lafon, who joined Jean-Michel Frank in the hit parade of chic. All this happened to the detriment of "minor 18th-century pieces" which were of interest only to the European new rich, incapable of finding their way among such diversity. The Givenchy sale nevertheless reminded the wider public of the persistance of great taste which also become more europeanized. Items originating in Augsburg are just as prestigious as those from Paris. Italian furniture, thanks to the scholarly work of the specialist Alvar Gonzales Palacios, finally became popular in France.

On the eve of its centennial, French Art Nouveau has returned to favor and, in the face of European competition, has proven to be the most refined, both in its forms and in its neurotic imagery, a vision anticipating the Surrealists. There has also been a recent revival of 19th-century furniture and a likely renewal of High Curiosity which, after having got lost for years in the *Haute Époque* furniture, has now become part of a search, through personalities such as Guy Ladrière or Philippe Carlier, for rare pieces of museum quality. Nowadays, it is hard to say what is in fashion. Or more precisely, it is impossible to say what is not in fashion, so ecumenical is the modern movement. Even kitsch itself has become a category of collectible. Everything seems to be worthy of interest and contemplation in contemporary eyes, which seem to bestow esthetic qualities upon every period of the past with the same liberality.

**MARCHÉ AUX PUCES
THE FLEA MARKET**
Booth of Nicolas Denis and Matthias Jousse. On the left, a white bed in fibreglass by Marc Eld. The upside down table-legs of the fibreglass table by Bertier (edition of the early 1970s). In the background, a wall cupboard made by Somop (1970s).

The Paris Biennale remains the greatest event of the antiques world, but its look has changed. As of the 1970s, the booths were integrated into a rigid framework which no longer has the flexibility and diversity of the beginnings. Wanting to distinguish themselves, some of the most important antique dealers of Paris, grouped under the title "Antiquaires de Paris," organized exceptional exhibitions at the Hôtel George V. At the 1986 Biennale, they confirmed their intention to stick together by taking a collective stand designed by François Cartroux. Two years later they disaffiliated with the Biennale and took over the Bagatelle castle, decorating it in homage to the Count of Artois. The Chinese pagoda built by Jacques Garcia for Jean Lupu in 1984, and the work of François-Joseph Graf, the antique dealers' favorite decorator, was a reminder that the decor was one of the Biennale's traditional attractions. The invitation extended in 1992 to Pier Luigi Pizzi, who had begun to create decors for art exhibitions, gave a more palatial air to the Grand Palais. The transfer of the event to the unattractive underground level of the Grand Louvre has had the paradoxical effect of causing antique dealers to attempt to emphasize the difference between their booths. Here, again, the work of François-Joseph Graf, joined by Pierre Hervé Walbaum or architects such as Richard Peduzzi, distinguishes itself. Today, many antique dealers prefer to concentrate their work on their showrooms and the budget that was once spent on the Biennale is now used for individual exhibitions for which catalogues are printed.

Indeed, the profile of the antique dealer has evolved immensely. In the 19th century, he had much in common with a manufacturer and a restorer. In the late 19th century, he held receptions like an aristocrat and started his career as a decorator. At the end of the 20th century, he became an art historian, and the presence of a well-stocked library was more reassuring to the client than the display of past glories. Documentation became an indispensable tool for knowledge, especially in regard to the 20th century domain, for which the Forney Library and that of the Decorative Arts Museum have become the best centers of learning for today's dealers of antiques of the modern era. The profusion of sales catalogues as well as the desire of collectors to learn more and more in an area which was long neglected by art historians requires the dealers to do their own research or hire a team of documentalists and researchers who haunt the shelves of the National Archives. On-the-job training is now supplemented by higher education: the new generation of dealers has usually been educated at the École du Louvre as well as at the university. Some, such as Bill G. B. Pallot, Didier Aaron's right-hand man, even teach at the Sorbonne. As art historians, they have sometimes turned to publishing or support art publications. For instance, the *Association des Antiquaires à Paris* published monographs on *La Folie d'Artois,* Maurice Segoura the work of Patricia Lemonnier on Weisweiler, or Jean Gismondi, *L'art du siège au XVIIIe siècle* by Bill G. B. Pallot. Most of all, dealers such as Didier Aaron, the Kugel brothers and Ariane Dandois organize exhibitions for which they publish catalogues. Catalogues produced for the Biennales with the photographs of the objects on display, accompanied by essays, are as heavy as exhibition catalogues. However, it is dealers, with their systematic policy of reviving the great unknowns, who have done the most to ensure the perpetuity of applied art of the 20th century. Names such as André Arbus, Jean-Charles Moreux, and Maxime Old and the decorators of the 1940s would never have been heard of again without Yves Gastou's efforts in publication and exhibition. Thanks to Philippe Jousse and Patrick Seguin, Jean Prouvé has also gained a new following amongst collectors of odern and contemporary art. The initiative of the galleries, attracting attention to a creator, often encouraged institutions to commit to 20th-century revivals. This was done by Antoine Broccardo in the case of Russian Art Nouveau, Anne-Sophie Duval with Armand-Albert Rateau, Thierry Bosselet with Carlo Mollino, Rafael Ortiz, Christian Boutonnet, and Pierre Passebon with Emilio Terry, Pierre Passebon again and Jacques Lacoste with Jean Royère, and Jean-Jacques Dutko with Eugène Printz. The colloquium on Hector Guimard organized by the Orsay Museum in 1992 rightly paid homage to Alain Blondel and Yves Plantin as pioneers and preservationists.

KUGEL GALLERY
The library on the second floor
of the gallery, Rue St. Honoré.

Another similarity brings the 20th century antique dealer and the gallery owner together: they both like to promote contemporary creativity and, above all, have the same customers.

Although the map of Parisian antique dealers had been set in stone since the 1920's, the last twenty years of the 20th century have seen it change. The installation of the Hôtel Drouot in the late 1970s relaunched the area around the Quai Voltaire and adjacent streets in which antiques stores pushed out the smaller businesses. But the success of *prêt-à-porter* boutiques was fatal to the extremities of the Left Bank, between Montparnasse and Saint-Germain-des-Prés. The Rue du Cherche-Midi, the Rue de Grenelle and the northern end of the Rue des Saints-Pères have been abandoned, even the Boulevard Saint-Germain has succumbed and all the activity is now concentrated on what is now called the Carré Rive Gauche and its immediate surroundings, from the quayside to the Rue de l'Université. A sense for curios, a certain eclecticism and an inclination for decor and confrontation have made this district one of the centers for antique-hunting, and it has become a favorite place for provincial dealers or traders from the flea market. The modern art galleries in Saint-Germain-des-Prés moved to the Beaubourg area in the late 1970s and were replaced by the first sellers of Art Nouveau and Art Deco, who were moving out of Les Halles and the Marché aux Puces. Today, the Rue de Seine and the Rue Bonaparte are the main arteries for 20th-century antiques, but stores can also be found near the Palais-Royal and the Bastille. The movement away from the Left Bank has favored the Faubourg Saint-Honoré which, since it is close to the big hotels and saleroom headquarters, has become the major axis of the top end of the market, to the detriment of the Quai Voltaire. The area around the Parc Monceau has retained a few exclusive establishments who resist the charms of the display window and indicate their presence by a mere plaque on the front of the building. But the fashionable neighborhoods are not what they used to be. The important antique dealers have abandoned the 16th arrondissement and the well-to-do no longer invest in 18th-century furniture, which is now beyond their means. Travel and financial investment have replaced expenditure and investment in antique furniture.

The new, affluent generation is leaving the stifling environment of Passy for the excitement of the "east-end." It is in the latter direction that dealers are now migrating, from Bastille right up to Ménilmontant. The first dealers in industrial furniture and tubular Art Deco have already opened their stores, followed by the promoters of the incunabula of Prouvé, Charlotte Perriand or Le Corbusier, like Philippe Jousse and Patick Seguin on the Rue de Charonne. On the same street, the first dealer in painted Provence furniture has set up between a trendy café and a dealer in chair frames of the "Faubourg" (furniture district). Already a few young dealers in oriental and African antiques have migrated to the Rue Oberkampf. We can be sure that the very day a luxury hotel whose guests include the fashionable crowd is built within the Bastille-République-Nation triangle, Faubourg Saint-Antoine will oust the Faubourg Saint-Honoré.

MADELEINE CASTAING'S APARTMENT located above her shop at the corner of the Rue Jacob and the Rue Bonaparte.

CHAPTER 2

THE
CLASSICS

DIDIER AARON
Didier Aaron & Cie, 8ᵉ arr.

Didier Aaron's future was all mapped out for him: "My father was a lawyer who became a banker and wanted me to become a financial controller. My mother held an antique store." Today, he and his son Hervé have about 30 employees, with a branch in London and another in New York. "My mother was the best friend of Marie Laurencin, the painter; her social circle contained nothing but painters, art dealers, and couturiers. On Wednesdays, I used to see Jean-Michel Frank, Georges Geffroy, Gérard Mille, Christian Bérard, and André Ostier. My mother's store, which was called *Chine France,* introduced me to Asian art objects."

Didier Aaron's formal education was interrupted by World War II, but he studied art history on his own. After the Liberation, he traded in antiques, first working from home then founding a firm of interior decorators which Alain Demachy then Jacques Grange would later join.

In the early 70s, he moved to Avenue Raymond Poincaré, where decoration was alotted the very top floor, great 18th centruy took over the upper floors, and paintings and drawings–in the charge of Henri Robert and Olivier Aaron could be seen on the ground floor.

In the late 80s, he moved into a town house on the Faubourg St. Honoré and decided to specialize: although he still presents objects and furniture in a carefully-prepared setting, the paintings and drawings earn a room of their own, where connoisseurs, collectors and museum curators can feel at home.

"Lovers of paintings do not like to be distracted. I remember an American client who had just bought a large Hubert Robert but was unpleasantly surprised to see a small 1900 sculpture on my premises; she immediately asked me for a certificate from another expert before accepting the canvas."

Didier Aaron continued to buy whatever he particularly liked, but Chinese and Japanese-style objects, exotica and 19th-century furniture tended to be relegated to warehouses at the Porte des Lilas. Only "serious" merchandise is acceptable in the store in the Faubourg, a policy which was reinforced when the next generation joined the firm. The younger set includes Bill G. B. Pallot, in charge of the furniture together with Lise Guénot and Véronique de Croisilles, is the son of an antique dealer, author of several works about 18th-century chairs, and teaches Decorative Arts at the Sorbonne; Bruno Desmaret, responsible for the paintings and drawings with

AARON
A roll-top secretary with violet wood, rose wood and amaranth marquetry, adorned with ormolu, stamped André-Antoine Lardin and Jean Mathieu Chevallier, Paris, circa 1750. *Portrait of the Marquise de Rânes,* by Nattier, circa 1740.

AARON

Above: In the drawing exhibition room of the gallery, the red chalk *Portrait d'homme* by Jean-Jacques de Boissieu
is standing against an easel. Against the table, *Jeunes Artistes sortant d'une propriété* by Jean-Antoine Alavoine.
Opposite: Table-desk with mobile tier in mahagony, ebony and burr yew on an oak frame.
Stamped by Adam Weisweiler, Paris, circa 1790.

Françoise Risso and Laure Pouzol; and Allan Salz, who presents paintings and drawings in New York.

Aaron's insistence on quality is combined with a love of rare pieces: a commode with six feet, a love-seat, and a French Empire double desk with six drawers. He also has a predilection for objects that are atypical, such as a desk by Weisweiler, which has an Art Deco feel with its burr veneer and lemonwood drawers, or an ambigous console stamped B.V.R.B. (Bernard (II) Vanrisamburgh), which appears to be a composite, since the feet are Louis XVI but the neo-classical decoration is rather naive in style. "Of course we have traditional merchandise, plain and simple Louis XV for clients who are setting up their home," explains Bill Palot, "but we would never stock commodes with flower marquetry or *bonheurs-du-jour.*" Under his influence, Didier Aaron indulged in his natural taste for the unusual chair, even an individual one, for the "item of sculpture." In the 1970s, Didier Aaron went in for large neo-classical pieces of furniture by David Roentgen with their strict architectural features. He also favored the best in European furniture, such as a Piedmontese green and gold lacquered table, Dutch console tables in the style of Daniel Marot, and pietra dura table tops (usually the early 19th-century examples rather than 17th-century). Here and there, a few pieces of Chinese porcelain, compositions of heterogenous elements, and jade continue in the tradition of *Chine France.*

In his apartment, Didier Aaron is not just an antique dealer. Fragonard hangs alongside Jean-Pierre Raynaud, Carrier-Belleuse stands next to Arman—but a most unusual Arman: an 18th-century armchair burned to a crisp! Which might have well pleased Philippe Jullian, the author of *Mémoires d'une Bergère.*

EUGÈNE BECKER

Eugène Becker, 8ᵉ arr.

Placed like a missal on a lectern, a thick quarto manuscript contains columns of text and figures. It is the inventory made of the collection of Hervart, Louis XIV's financier, after his death. Paragraph after paragraph list the objects and furniture owned by one of the wealthiest men of his age, psalms or litanies to possessions which one longs to read out loud. "A Boulle marquetry chest, decorated with two golden masks… a cabinet inlaid with pietra dura." "It is like watching an old film, where some images jump out and hit you. Through this austere prose, one can suddenly grasp a slice of life," Eugène Becker explains.

Eugène and Marie-Louise Becker began their venture in the 1970s with a store in the Marais district they bought to occupy a friend who was looking for something to do. The Beckers were in the course of furnishing their country retreat and began serious antique-hunting. They became caught up in the game, concentrating on the kind of "good quality" furniture that other young households would like. At the time, the Marais was becoming fashionable again and Haute Epoque "shabby chic" furniture was selling quite well. But the pleasure of playing at storekeeping was soon overtaken by Eugene's desire to approach the business seriously. As a graduate of a military academy who went on to earn degrees in chemistry, he had a reputation for a strong mathematical bent, which he felt was limiting. Antiques gave him an interest in history which he methodically researched. He would pore over sale catalogues, then volumes of documents at the French National Archives and the unending lists of the inventories. In this way, he discovered his famous predecessors such as Pierre Verlet, who would relentlessly research royal origins, and Bruno Pons.

Eugène Becker was one of the first of the new generation of dealers to integrate art history into his work. "I believe that each era relives the past in its own way. From the 19th century through the 1950s, people wanted to recreate a period interior. Today, people dream of owning an important item, something with a pedigree.

BECKER

On each side of the table signed "RVLC," two armchairs by Jacob for the Duke of Penthièvre, bearing the mark of his castle in Châteauneuf. The white and blue biscuit clock "à l'Uranie" comes from the manufactory of the Duke of Angoulême. Both plaster model figurines are by Falconnet. The terra cotta bas relief is late 18th century.

People no longer ask themselves, 'Would this fit in my home?' but 'Is this item of museum quality?'" This vision applies to furniture, as well as to objects hitherto considered decoration, such as large porcelain objects commissioned by the French royal family or wealthy financiers, terra cotta, and bronzes. He also likes architectural and unusual furniture, "such as Boulle furniture which does not have Boulle marquetry," chairs of an interesting shape. He prefers displaying their scarred frames rather than covering them with rich silk upholstery. There are few paintings but there are drawings which are connected with decorative art, such as ornament drawings for objects and paneling. Marie-Louise Becker is currently studying the work of Marie-Anne Collot, whose terra cotta sculptures featured in all the major collections of the 19th century.

The Beckers' love of meticulous research is not confined to exploring libraries. Eugène Becker loves to go and discover and buy. "The main thing, above all, is taking a critical look. It's the confrontation of different appraisals of an item. That's where the contact with our customers is important—their final evaluation of our choices helps us keep our feet on the ground."

ARIANE DANDOIS

Ariane Dandois, 8ᵉ arr.

Ariane Dandois is a former journalist at *France Soir,* and press agent for Port-Grimaud. She came to antique dealing at the age of twenty-eight. "For ten years, I attended endless courses at Guimet. I was interested in everything, a dilettante, with that frenzy for work which is the prerogative of the lazy." The trigger was a visit to the King's Road in London, where she discovered a Japanese screen with bamboo in a shop window. Inside, on a table, there was a tantric design. "I have another five hundred of them," the owner told her. There was an immediate bond between them. "Jean-Claude Ciancimino is a creator, designer, and a potter. We both love contemporary art, and that's what caused us to love Japanese art. That very evening, I asked him if he wanted to open a gallery with me in Paris."

The store was on the Rue des Saints-Pères, and opened in 1973. The showroom exhibited Japanese screens, lacquerwork, bronzes, sculptures from northern India, but no archeological artefacts. "Nicolas Landau used to go by the store every day. One day, he came in and bought a small Japanese bronze for 5,000 francs. He returned a few days later to inform me that he had just resold it for 100,000. 'I am not telling you this to teach you the job, but to encourage you to learn more about what you have.' I was mortified, but had learned a good lesson all the same."

A first exhibition on tantric art whose geometrical diagrams are similar to those of abstract art then a display of Ming furniture confirmed this modern esthetic. On a trip to Rajasthan, Dandois discovered a set of marble furniture stacked up in the hunting lodge of the Maharaja of Bikaner. "Would you agree to sell it?" "Only if you take it all," replied the present owner. It took more than one eventful year to restore and move the tons of white marble.

Even more memorable was the exhibition of Japanese screens, "with three successive hangings of eighteen screens." Then came the fateful day on which the famous French author Marguerite Yourcenar entered the gallery. "I couldn't believe my eyes, I thought I was having hallucinations. She went toward a Genji scene and began to talk to me, and then I showed her the legend which bore her name and the title of *Nouvelles orientales.*"

In the early 1980s, there was a change of style in favor of something more conventional. "I had done the rounds of Far Eastern art. Taste changes. And in any case, everything had become rare and inaccessible." So she began

DANDOIS

Opposite: In her new gallery on the Faubourg St. Honoré, Ariane Dandois has chosen to show objects and furniture of the 18th and 19th century in a plain and sober setting in order to highlight them. The Venetian rococo mirror and the painted panels decorated with neoclassical grotesques show the eclecticism of her choices.

(following pages)
DANDOIS
In the drawing room on the second floor, the Italian neoclassical mantelpiece and the pair of mahogany female sphinxes set the tone. A set of neoclassical chairs by Kaeshammer (Strasbourg, 1780) is spread throughout the room. The big pedestal table in the foreground is French Empire.

to discover neo-classical European furniture, all of it as far removed from Parisian style as possible, with its lightness, freedom, and daring. The first stage was Russia: "My mother was Russian and my father half-Nordic, so I was sort of returning to my roots." After Russia came Sweden, then Austria and its Biedermeier. There was mahogany and ormolu, as well as pale woods, burr veneer, large porcelain vases, sculpture and a quest for the big names such as Thomas Hope and Karl Friedrich Schinkel. Dandois tries to keep some of the handsomest pieces for herself–"it's what I call the right of finder's keepers"—combining them with the work of her favorite artists, Germaine Richier, Jean Dubuffet, Joan Miró, and a few Symbolists such as Burne-Jones and Dante Gabriel Rossetti.

Dandois moved her store to the Faubourg Saint-Honoré in 1999. She decided to make the new gallery into a space that was neutral and abstract, where the furniture and objects would speak for themselves. Two exhibitions devoted to painted Italian furniture and European Empire furniture asserted her attachment to European style, though one display case is still reserved for the Far East, a reminder of her first love.

FRANÇOIS FABIUS

Fabius Frères, 8ᵉ arr.

Fabius Frères is an institution, one of the last firms to remain loyal to the Plaine Monceau. This neighborhood first became popular with antique dealers in the early 20th century, when many of them, like Fabius, moved out of the Drouot district. "From the very beginning of the 20th century, they dealt in all types of antiques, as was the custom at the time. There was just about everything: furniture, art objects, paintings, and sculptures, ranging in period from the 17th to the early 20th century but whatever the period, the emphasis was on the unusual, the rare, and the quality. That is what they sought. And they always used Barye and Carpeaux as the principal artists." "They" refers to the three Fabius brothers, André, François' father and his two uncles, Fernand and Pierre, who still put in an appearance from time to time—and also includes their grandfather Elie who had started on the Rue de Provence in 1885. Unfortunately, the continuity was interrupted by the German occupation, with the appointment of *commissaires-gérants* and numerous forced sales at the Drouot auction rooms which lasted for a whole week. This was too much for the grandfather. In 1945, the three Fabius brothers reopened for business on the Boulevard Haussmann: "Fabius Frères, 18th century and First Empire furniture, pictures, sculpture, historic objects."

François Fabius hesitated for a moment as to whether to follow the family business. He studied law for a while but his passion for competitive horsemanship and various travels got in the way. He eventually came back to the family business and had a dual apprenticeship in the trade, working in the showroom while studying at the École du Louvre.

Had he followed in the family tradition? Fairplay, François Fabius dodges the question: "I am slightly in the family tradition, but personally I love the 19th century." Which is certainly clear enough. He also likes the work of the two "house artists," Barye et Carpeaux. Here, François Fabius is benefitting from family experience which was passed on during daily visits to the Drouot auction rooms or to museums, to see works of art and learn how they are made, their history and legends. Even better yet to discover the elusive ones. "It is amusing to find objects or sculptures in a field with which one is very familiar that were thought to have been lost, such as this *Amazone* by Barye, a magnificent bronze. I had never seen an original cast of it. I don't think my father ever saw it, nor my grandfather. When I found it not so long ago, I couldn't believe my eyes."

FABIUS
Jean-Baptiste Carpeaux: *La Palombella,* original plaster, *Bacchante aux roses,* terra cotta, *Ugolin,* original plaster, *Le Printemps,* terra cotta, *La Candeur,* original plaster. On the wall, *Vue du château de Fontainebleau* by Bouhot, *Portrait du docteur Louis* by Duplessis and two 18th-century chinoiseries. Gilt wooden chairs by Othon, 18th century.

His passion for sculpture led François Fabius to become interested in such 20th-century artists as Mateo Hernandez, who works by carving stone directly, but he continues the "encyclopedic" tradition of the Fabius firm, dealing in large and small format paintings, historical objects such as the Sèvres vases, a gift from Napoleon to his brother Jerome, and modern glassware. There is also furniture of the highest quality, collector's items, furniture made by artists, such as a writing table by Montigny or Levasseur, marked with a Medusa's head, a chest of drawers by Riesener that has forgotten to be royal, an Empire side-table which Mario Praz would have liked, a satin-finish chest of drawers by Boulle with boxwood bands, and a stylish secretary by Topino. Although at one time he was tempted to join his colleagues in the Faubourg Saint Honoré, François Fabius remains faithful to the original address. "The address has become known and it's easy toget to," a location that is convenient after a visit to the Jacquemard-André or Nissim de Camondo museums, two other witnesses to the greatness of the Plaine Monceau.

MICHEL AND JEAN-PAUL FABRE

Fabre et Fils, 8ᵉ arr.

There have always been two Fabre brothers. Basile, the grandfather, had a store at 68, Rue de Rennes in 1898, and his brother Augustin, known as "le petit Fabre," was at 17, Rue du Cherche-Midi. Then came Paul Fabre, who established himself on the Avenue de Tourville, and was joined by André. Both of them crossed the Seine in 1924 to make the Plaine Monceau their headquarters. The store on the Rue Balzac is currently run by Jean-Paul and his brother Michel. "My grandfather was born in 1854, the eldest of six children. His parents were farmers in Lozère." One day, the owners of a castle, instead of paying cash, paid him with an 18th-century tapestry. Realizing he could resell it for a handsome sum, Basile Fabre decided to move to Paris. "He knew nothing about the trade." It was a time when the inhabitants of this far-flung region–the Auvergnats–came to Paris to try their hand as junk vendors or bar owners.

His beginnings were modest. He saved every penny, traveled third class, spent nights in station waiting rooms, carrying the furniture he purchased on his back. Basile Fabre always kept the penny-pinching habits from this period of his life, which made his fellow antique dealers smile. In the initial stages he sold country furniture which he displayed on the Rue de Rennes, much of it on the sidewalk. He went on to buy "more Parisian stuff," but it was Uncle Paul who took the firm forward into the "high 18th-century," at a time of major English country house sales. The mansion on the Rue Balzac is proof of this new prosperity. Its three stories are used as a showroom, a large hall and a grand staircase to display marbles and sculptures. High-ceilinged reception rooms house the large items of furniture, the chairs, tapestries, woodwork, and bookcases. There is no fancy decor or spotlights, just room in which to view the artefacts of the Ancien Régime, presented in close ranks. "I was raised on strict principles: mahogany was banished and the Empire style was only good enough for dentists. Some of our clients even found Louis XVI to be of dubious taste. The great French taste was for Louis XV. It was not until the 1960s, with decorators such as Georges Geffroy and dealers such as Jean-Pierre Hagnauer, that things began to change."

Not only are the Fabres a family of antique dealers, they are family antique dealers, since some of the clients have been with them for generations, as if they were family lawyers or doctors. This is due to their solid reputation. "'I have never had to cross the road to avoid meeting a client,' my grandfather used to say." This trust facilitates discreet transactions, far from the spotlights of the auction rooms, and explains Jean-Paul Fabre's role as an expert, who these days privileges purchases "at the source." "Apart from our trips to England, I used to

FABRE
Opposite: Marquetry and ormolu scrolled secretary, stamped RVLC, period of Louis XV. Beauvais tapestry, 18th century, *Apollo and the python snake.*

(following pages)
FABRE
Left: Diane au bain (statue in stone, France, 18th century). In the foreground: colored marble marquetry tabletop (Italy, late 16th century). On the landing, tall terra cotta Médici vase of the 18th century, adorned with a bacchanalia. *Right:* In the hall, busts of Roman Emperors and two Medici vases in white marble, 18th century.

hunt for antiques with my father in the mornings on the Rue du Cherche-Midi and at the Drouot auction house; in the afternoon, we would receive clients." Curators and decorators have long replaced the internationally famous dealers such as Duveen and Hans Stiebel, but the clientele has basically remained unchanged. These customers do not need long explanations, references, or elaborate settings in order to feel reassured. The only difference, which is due both to the increasing rarity of the merchandise and the personal taste of Jean-Paul Fabre, is a preference for specially commissioned furniture that is out of the ordinary, furniture that is a work of art in itself and is reserved for connoisseurs. "I have decided to take only an interest in what I really like," explains Jean-Paul Fabre, who has also decided, together with his brother, to concentrate the firm's activity in the firm's mansion.

JEAN GISMONDI

Gismondi, 8ᵉ arr.

Jean Gismondi is a true southerner. He studied at the École des Beaux-Arts in Nice, then did internships with various architects which brought him into contact with interior design. He began looking for objects and architectural elements of facades. He also discovered modern art from the many artists living in the region and from such great connoisseurs as Aimé Maeght. At the age of twenty, he sold his sub-compact car to buy his first Braque, Miró, Bram Van Velde, and Giacometti prints. Antique-hunting and modern art have remained his two passions. After his father's death, he began sculpting in wood, but to earn a livelihood he bought a store on the ramparts of old Antibes where he displayed Provençal bare wooden furniture. In Beaulieu, which was an important antiques center, he discovered a pietra dura marquetry cabinet and learned that it cost three times less than a run-of-the-mill Louis XV chest of drawers.

"My training as an architect enabled me to appreciate such objects which were underrated at the time." He was attracted by the ingeniousness of marquetry, in wood, and later in pietra dura, as well as the intricate Boulle marquetry which was also undervalued at the time. "On the Riviera, we are a long way from the Louvre and the best examples. It is only when I opened a restoration and repair workshop that I deepened my knowledge of the trade, thanks to the fabulous skilled craftsmen who worked for me. You understand everything when a piece of furniture is stripped down." Jean Gismondi retained his contacts in artistic circles, especially with César, who initiated him into the techniques of compression. "He lived in my home for two years. It's really quite something, living with a genius. When he explained something, he drew it in words. Through him and Arman, I discovered polyester, and it gave me the idea of creating bases for my cabinets." It was a clever way of introducing very architectural furniture into the modern decor of the 1970s, like mysterious objects which seemed to float under spotlights. This adaptation of an old piece to modern decor or modern art to a traditional decor is one of the constants of the Gismondi style. Gismondi took over Maurice and Marion Bensimon's boutique in 1981. Bensimon had been one of the big dealers in "good 18th-century", on the Rue Royale in Paris, but Gismondi decided to exhibit his favorite artists there as well, French Realists and New German Expressionists such as Fetting, Castelli, and Salomé, whose colors set off the red tortoiseshell, ebony, and ivory of the cabinets. Does Gismondi tend toward interior decoration? "There is something of that in my training, but I am not a decorator. I work with professionals, such as Guy Marie Kiefer, but I prefer to be in charge of an entire project." Examples of this are the apartment owned by Marina Picasso, or that of Catherine and Michel Pastor where Gismondi, in collaboration with Garouste and Bonetti and the Galerie Neotu, has recently redecorated in

GISMONDI
In the foreground, a carved and gilt wooden armchair, Louis XIV period. On the Boulle desk, Louis XIV period, a brown patina bronze *Amphitrite,* after Michel Anguier, early 18th century.

GISMONDI

Above: On the Boulle secretary, three superposed cabinets: red and ivory tortoiseshell, Indo-Portuguese, 17th century; red and gilt copper tortoiseshell, Antwerpian, 17th century; ebony, attributed to Jacobo Flamengo, adorned with engraved ivory plates. *Opposite:* On a console table made circa 1768 for Louis XV, a pair of candelabras supported by hard paste biscuit vestals *à l'antique* from the Sèvres porcelain factory, Louis XVI. Chinese celadon vase (Kianlong period, 1736-1796), mounted on Louis XV ormolu.

contemporary style with a Combas ceiling. Gismondi's arrival in Paris was the occasion for expansion into other types of furniture. "I like cabinets with spectacular facades, as well as modifiable furniture or very handsome chairs." It is this recent enthusiasm which has led Gismondi to co-publish with ACR Bill G. B. Pallot's book, *The Art of the 18th-Century Chair in France.* But Jean Gismondi is not an unconditional enthusiast for "good 18th-century." He continues to run his showroom in Antibes and remains faithful to his first loves.

MARCEL GRUNSPAN

Marcel Grunspan, 8ᵉ arr.

Marcel Grunspan, his son Pierre, and his niece, Annie Partouche, are the incarnation of a family business in Parisian antique dealing that can trace its roots back several generations. In 1900, Grandmother Grunspan had a second-hand dealershop on the Rue du Cardinal-Lemoine. Her son Émile opened a store in 1924 on the Rue Saint-Louis-en-l'Île, where he displayed "good 18th-century and Empire furniture." His clientele consisted mainly of merchants and lawyers who would linger in this street that bisected what was then a working-class neighborhood not far from their apartments along the Seine. Émile Grunspan loved painting and he attended the sale of the Schuffenecker estate. During the Occupation, he went underground when his wife was deported, then re-opened his store after the War. Marcel followed in his father's footsteps, but chose to deal in earlier objects–acquiring furniture by André-Charles Boulle and Pierre Gole–and specialized in old scientific instruments. He set up shop in Beaulieu in 1952, when antique dealing was booming thanks to an international clientele and the twilight era of the great villas, which included the treasures of Somerset Maugham and the Art Deco objects of Maurice Maeterlinck's *Villa Orlamonde.*

It is at this point that Annie Partouche enters the story. She had taken a year's unpaid leave from her job at the *Centre National de Recherche Scientifique* to learn more about the still-discredited Art Nouveau and Art Deco periods. After long days spent in the Forney and the Decorative Arts Museum libraries, she went ahead and bought what she liked, much to the stupefaction of her colleagues. Her acquisitions included lacquerware by Jean Dunand, carpets by Ivan Da Silva Bruhns and *pâte-de-verre* by Argy Rousseau. "Besides old magazines, no other documentation existed at the time. You just had to trust your own intuition."

The store on the Rue de Provence enabled Marcel and Annie to remain at the heart of the market. Although Marcel, like his father, loved "high 18th-century," Annie instinctively chose "high Art Deco." Her purchases include a large Eileen Gray console table in raspberry red with a gold band, and a screen "that was painted in tortoiseshell lacquer, semi-transparent and lovely as an abstract painting," then Pierre Legrain and Jean-Michel Frank whose work in straw, fishskin, and parchment was affordable in the late 1970s. "I love the purity of the lines, the proportions, the balance, but I am also sensitive to lovely materials."

In 1981, Marcel Grunspan and Annie Partouche set up shop on the Rue Royale, in the courtyard of the former Town House of Madame de Staël. The first floor was dedicated to Art Deco and a series of salons on the upper floor were in 18th-century style. Art Deco is currently displayed in the store window overlooking the street and the showroom in the courtyard has a look which Grandma Grunspan would probably have liked. The vast entrance hall dominated by a spectacular stone staircase is furnished with a few Empire or Italian baroque pieces and a large screen. On the landing there are some 17th-century cabinets. The apartments on the upper floors enhance the 18th-century furniture and large tapestries, while the small reception rooms have been converted into a "castle bedroom," a cabinet of scientific curiosities and a cabinet of drawings, a new

GRUNSPAN

Opposite: A Chinese gilt lacquer screen by Jean Dunand, decorated by Jean Lambert Rucki (1928), standing behind a light walnut octogonal tabletop attributed to Dominique, circa 1930.

(following pages)
GRUNSPAN

Four carved silver Venetian grotto chairs, (1800-1850). Behind the carved Regency console table, a 12-panel Coromandel lacquer screen (China, late 17th century). Gilded wooden chandelier, North Italy, 18th century.

speciality presented by Pierre Grunspan and Gabriel Terrades. The casual style of presentation and the nobility of the surroundings are evocative of how an important antique dealer would be set up in the provinces—in a mansion, near the cathedral, in harmony with its chiming bells. Far from the bustle of the inner city, it is a privileged haven to which decorators from all over the world are in the habit of bringing their clients.

ALEXIS AND NICOLAS KUGEL
J. Kugel, 8ᵉ arr.

"When, some months after the death of our father, we bought a bronze microscope attributed to Caffieri in Monaco, for which we paid four times the estimated value, and sold it only a month later to the Getty Museum, people in the trade realized that the firm was in safe hands," Alexis and Nicolas Kugel explain. When aged 22 and 19 years old respectively, they had a hard time taking over from their father, Jacques Kugel, one of the great dealers in what were once called "curiosities." Kugel was both an eminent scholar and great businessman, who liked to operate as a one-man band, keeping his trade secrets close to his chest.

"Dad wasn't much of a teacher," recalls Alexis who nevertheless chose to go into the family business and study at the École du Louvre. "He rarely took us to auction houses," adds Nicolas, who began a career in movie-making, avoiding the antique trade which he swore never to embrace. When Kugel Sr. died prematurely in 1985, however, his heirs were forced to take over the business. "We were fortunate in having a fairly prosperous period in which to learn the basics without doing too much damage and everything followed on from there quite naturally."

They first exhibited at the Antiques Biennale in 1988. Their booth was modern, ensheathed in metal, and displayed small, valuable items such as tobacco-boxes, gold medals, mounted hardstone gems, and carved ivories floating against a black background under fiber-optic lighting. The whole display was stunning in its richness and audacity. "They are selling off their father's prize possessions," went the rumor. "When we explained that this Biennale was the product of our own purchases, people were almost disappointed; so we just let the rumors buzz."

With this modern cabinet of curiosities, Alexis and Nicolas, whose Russian names are a reminder of the origin of their father, Jacques Kugel, are following in their father's footsteps and his international quest for treasures. The Ambras treasury and the Green Vault of Dresden were as familiar to him as the Apollo Galleries or the royal apartments of Versailles. He could have offered advice to Rudolph II or William Beckford, being as familiar with silver seals as with the royal faces in anonymous miniatures.

At their second Biennale, the change was even more apparent. Alexis and Nicolas showed two Boulle closets and a collection of Limoges enamel bought directly from Hubert de Givenchy outside the auction of his collection. As a sign of his friendship and esteem, Givenchy designed the booth in green velvet which served as a sumptuous backdrop to Augsburg wall lamps , large bronzes, and the black and gold Boulle furniture. It was a victory for grand European taste over good French style. The collection was recorded in two magnificent catalogs.

Since then the two brothers have concentrated their activities on their gallery and during the Biennales they organize thematic exhibits—*Views of Paris, Treasures from Russia* or *Jewels of the Renaissance*—which are always accompanied by catalogs. For the rest of the year, the Kugel gallery returns to its traditional display. An antechamber is devoted to silver and porcelain, then there is a marble gallery for monumental sculpture and other

KUGEL

Above: The marquetry bookcase from the Versailles castle is attributed to Joseph Baumhauer (France, 1750). The stoneware falcons, partly enameled, are Japanese 19th century. *Opposite:* A pair of globes by Matthaus Greuter, produced by Dominici Rubéis (Rome, 1695). On a pietra dura marquetry tabletop (Naples, circa 1660), with a base by Emilio Terry, stands a black marble and jasper Roman bust (c. 1600), two peacocks made from ostrich eggs (Italy, c. 1600). The *Mercure and Argus* bronze is by Giovanni Battista Foggini (Florence, late 17th century). Jasper bowl by J.M. Meyer (Augsburg, c. 1650).

huge pieces, leading into the green drawing room which contains 17th and 18th-century furniture. A spiral staircase leads to the floor below with its walls sheathed in red, reserved for curios, Renaissance cabinets, porcelain and small bronzes. The overwhelming diversity and profusion may prove too much for the novice who has entered the store merely to acquire a few items of furniture. But rest assured: despite their international trade, the two brothers take turns manning the store and are always there to welcome and guide you with a courtesy that is just as much a part of their inheritance.

JEAN LUPU

Jean Lupu, 8ᵉ arr.

Jean Lupu's move from the Faubourg Saint-Antoine, where his father owned an antique restoration workshop to his own mansion on the Faubourg Saint-Honoré is the story of a professional evolution with typical roots in Parisian cabinet-making and curio dealing.

"When I was a child, my father would take me to visit his workshop in the Rue d'Aligre, where there was an odor of sawdust and varnish which remains familiar to me. He also had a tiny shop which sold secondhand furniture." He studied cabinet-making at the Boulle School, which gave him the eye of an expert. Upon graduation, he took a booth at the flea market, the Marché aux Puces: "It was the time when the Louis-Philippe period was popular, but it was still possible to find genuine period furniture."

From there, Lupu moved to the fashionable 16th arrondissement "where most of my biggest clients lived. I bought a lot from private individuals and all the antique dealers of the Faubourg Saint-Honoré would come and see me."

The third stage was the Faubourg itself and, at the same time, a foothold on the Rue de Beaune. The more elegant merchandise on the Left Bank was intended for French collectors; the Right Bank establishment was grander and was aimed at an international clientele. "Anyone who is a financial success will turn up in Paris. Being interested in art objects is not just a matter of taste, it is a matter of social standing."

Jean Lupu still has a display window on the Faubourg, but he receives his favorite clients on the courtyard side, where a gallery and four main rooms spendidly redone by Jacques Garcia provide the perfect setting for his masterpieces. In the large Regency room, against a backdrop of antique paneling, four chests of drawers stand facing each other, flanked by armchairs, while another ring of chairs surrounds a writing table. A large Aubusson carpet covers the floor. The room is filled with biscuit, terra cotta and Sevres porcelain. It is a "challenge to taste," to repeat the title of an exhibition at the Louvre devoted to these works of art. Lupu tells the story of a gleaming chest of drawers decorated in tortoiseshell with ormolu "pagodas:" "At the Drouot auction rooms, it was described as 'in the style of,' perhaps because of the veneering, but I recognized the frame as being absolutely right for the period. Unfortunately, I wasn't the only one. After the sale, I still had the surprise of discovering part of the original tortoiseshell veneer." This superb piece, which has now been given to Noël Gérard, was restored to its original glory thanks to the restoration workshop that Lupu runs on the premises. "Having my restorers on tap enables me to supervise their work constantly and guide them. I favor precautionary restoration, which must be reversible and which respects the authenticity of the piece," explains this former student of the Boulle school. "I love large pieces of furniture, royal commissions or atypical pieces of which only a few were made," Jean Lupu explains. In addition to his great admiration for the masterpieces, he still has an affection for more modest craft woodworkers such as Roussel, "simple, naive, spontaneous, charming,

LUPU
In the main drawing room, between two windows, the Louis XVI Japanese lacquer secretary is attributed to Martin Carlin, circa 1780. The Louis XV Chinese lacquer desk is stamped J. Dubois, circa 1745-1749. On the mantelpiece, a Louis XVI biscuit clock from the manufactory of Sèvres with a decor of hunting scenes.

whose marquetry reflects the landscapes of France as it used to be."

His booths at the Biennales–a pyramid, a pagoda, a salon full of green plants–designed by Jacques Garcia, were always outstandingly original, but he decided he would no longer exhibit after the move to the Carrousel du Louvre. He continues to travel around the world in search of rarities then returns home to the Faubourg, where only an initiated few will be greeted in holy of holies.

JACQUES, PATRICK AND PHILIPPE PERRIN

Jacques and Patrick Perrin, 8ᵉ arr.; Philippe Perrin, 7ᵉ arr.

"I started antique dealing out of love," says Jacques Perrin whose great charm and sense of business have worked wonders. "Third generation in a family of antique dealers," he learned his trade on the job and swiftly recognized the significance of superior 18th-century French pieces in the market as high-quality artefacts coveted by collectors. Curators approve of his choices, as will attest the humpback desk stamped B.V.R.B. in Versailles, a pair of cases by Delafosse at the Getty Museum and a porcelain table by Carlin at the Metropolitan Museum of Art in New York.

But even the best merchandise in the world cannot be sold by an unknown.

"A new dealer must make a name for himself, acquire a reputation. When I first exhibited at the *Biennale des Antiquaires* in 1966, 70% of the artefacts I displayed had been lent to me by eminent colleagues (who hadn't wanted to participate at the time), few people ventured into my booth. They needed to ask around, find out who I was." Attentive to people's reactions, Jacques Perrin quickly realized that the image he projected was as precious as the objects in his showroom, and he was one of the first dealers to use the services of a press agent. He also learned that knowlege of art is worthless without a sensitivity to changes in taste, that the antique dealer must be ready to take on the role of an advisor knowing how to discern and satisfy the expectations of his clients and their decorator. Tactful and diplomatic, he rapidly became one of the key actors in the trade, serving as President of the Biennale and the "Antiquaires à Paris" group.

The end of the 1980s marked a turning point. He left the management of the gallery on the Quai Voltaire to his son Philippe, crossed the Seine and entered the Faubourg Saint-Honoré with his other son, Patrick, being one of the first to conquer the Place Beauvau.

The two brothers set about forging an international reputation and divide their time accordingly: Patrick goes to Maastricht, London and New York in October, Philippe to Monaco and New York in January. "Messieurs Perrin" are now known throughout the world. "The Dutch like plain furniture, mahagony, the German prefer marquetry, the Americans small pieces of furniture," they explain.

PERRIN
In the foreground, a caned, curve-backed armchair in untinted wood, 1750. The pair of gilt wooden Louis XV armchairs is stamped Delanois, 1750. On the columns, a pair of crackled celadon vases, China, Louis XVI ormolu mounting, circa 1775. On the wall, a Genoese mirror with carved wood frame, 1690. The 12-branch crystal chandelier is Swedish, 1790.

Having inherited his father's social sense, Patrick was in charge of organizing the *Salon du Dessin* then the *Pavillon des Antiquaires et des Beaux-Arts.* Philippe, whose eclectic tastes lead him to collect not only objects from the 18th century, but 20th-century furniture and contemporary art, has convinced his brother to include them in his expositions.

"Being the heirs to a great tradition," they are eager to pass it on. So they have decided to sponsor a series of theses on the great masters of cabinet-making of the 18th century, under the supervision of Thibault Wolvesperges, professor at the University of Paris IV, and with the blessings of museum curators. The first of these *Cahiers du mobilier* will be dedicated to Roger Van Der Cruse, called Lacroix, who is better known by his stamped initials: R.V.L.C. Studies on Leleu, Canabas and Topino will follow.

PERRIN

Opposite: In the foreground of the window display, a carved and gilt wooden center table with baluster legs, adorned with acanthus leaves
and putti, period of Louis XIV. Against the wall in the background, a mahogany Louis XVI bookcase and an Aubusson tapestry from the 17th century.
Above: Card table with rose and violet wood veneer, adorned with ormolus. The removeable tabletop reveals a backgammon game
with ebony, ivory and greencolored ivory veneer. Stamped P. Roussel, from the collection of Princess Rudolf de Lippe.

JEAN-MARIE ROSSI

Aveline, 8ᵉ arr.

After 45 years of experience at Aveline on the Rue du Cirque, Jean-Marie Rossi broke away and established his own store just a few steps away on the Place Beauvau, at the same address as the earlier shop held by Doucet, one of the famous names in the Faubourg around World War II. The establishment consists of several floors surrounding a palatial hall decorated with the favorite mottos of the owner of the house, *qualis artifex...*

Like all those who take their occupation seriously, Jean-Marie Rossi has always loved irony, humor, the out of phase. Although he is a great among greats, he has never clung to the fetish of good taste of the Faubourg-Saint-Honoré.

He is, above all, a "modernist" as revealed in the work that decorates his private office and in his choices for the collectors' exhibition entitled *Passions Privées* at the Musée d'Art Moderne de la Ville de Paris. In the 1970s, he and his friend Durand-Ruel even reproduced limited editions of decorative objects such as lamps by César and consoles by Hickquilly. "I have always been interested in what is happening today and that has always help-ed me, what Nicolas Landau used to call 'seeking the modern throughout the ages.' It is easier to discern the best of the 18th century when you know what preceded it or followed it. I prefer the avant-garde of every era: I would rather a Renaissance anatomical model in bronze than a Roman copy of a Greek bronze."

This taste for innovation and creation paradoxically explains his interest, for example, in large display pieces which graced the 19th-century World Fairs, the "neo-Merovingian" or "Japanese" ornamental monsters by Charles-Guillaume Diehl or Alfred Beurdeley, which he sells to the Orsay Museum or at the Metropolitan. In the 1970s, Rossi and his friend Albert Benamou made extensive purchases of large 19th-century pieces which were still despised as "*pompiers.*" The taste for excess and ostentation has steered this dealer of "grand 18th-century" away from anything small or conventional: "I don't buy small Louis XV marquetry furniture, little *bonheurs-du-jour,* sugary Louis XV or the affected piece with porcelain plaques, unless it is a masterpiece such as the chest of drawers by Carlin donated by Marie-Hélène de Rothschild to the Louvre or the jewel casket bought by Roberto Polo: and after all, two masterpieces, in the life of an antique dealer, is quite an achievement."

Rossi rediscovered at the same time as his friend Jean-Pierre Hagnauer the great architectural furniture by Roentgen, "Catherine II quality," as well as the Boulle chests of drawers which he bought in London in the 1950s, or from his major Parisian colleagues. "You couldn't sell Boulle at the time. Now you still can't sell it—because it's too expensive." There are large writing tables, corner cupboards encrusted with pietra dura and ormolu, palatial neo-classical console tables, monumental lamps—nothing paltry or average, and a real feeling for the quality of the materials, the ornamental detail, and the proportions. This has been greatly appreciated by museums such as the Getty and the Metropolitan and the important collectors of the 1960s, such as Antenor Patino or René Grog, whose purchases are now the pride of the Louvre, as well as those indispensable inter-mediaries for the beginning collector, interior designers such as Henri Samuel, Georges Geffroy, Victor Grandpierre, and Gérard Mille.

Has the market changed? Jean-Marie Rossi looks back regretfully at the passing of a race of cultivated collect-ors, from William Beckford to Arturo Lopez and Charles de Beistegui, who had a taste for the theatrical, for interpretation. But although the customers change, some of the objects come back, the same taste lingers on, as stated in the inscription on the Palazzo Rossi, *qualis artifex.*

MAURICE, MARC AND PIERRE SEGOURA

Segoura, 8ᵉ arr.

By locating his showroom on the Place François-Ier, just around the corner from the Avenue Montaigne, in the Hôtel de Clermont-Tonnerre with its opulent Second Empire architecture, Maurice Segoura joins the tradition of Seligman and Wildenstein, enhancing his collection by placing it in a setting that is worthy of it. The lavish decor borrows extensively from the 18th century and was restored by the decorator François-Joseph Graf, the vastness of the rooms allowing even the largest items of furniture and the most monumental objects to be comfortably displayed. Maurice Segoura loves "grand music," large royal objects and aristocratic commissions that have nothing classical about them. Examples are the desk by Jean-Henri Riesener intended for Versailles or the chest of drawers marked with the inventory numbers of the Tuileries palace. It is an enthusiasm he shares with his two sons, Pierre and Marc. "You can never hang on to a beautiful object" is a piece of advice well learned during his apprenticeship, alongside another: "Learn with your own money." "This is a very rough and demanding occupation, which is very trying in its early stages: you can make mistakes... expensive ones."

In this business where there are very few self-made men, Maurice Segoura was helped by his father-in-law, Braunstein, who had a store on the Boulevard de Courcelles called *Belles Époques.* He also learned the trade from the great names of the previous generation, Étienne Lévy and René Weiller, on the Rue Lammenais, for whom he was one of the outstanding antique-hunters. In 1968, he took over the business run by Yvonne de Brémond d'Ars, an antique dealer and novelist, whose store, "a window open on a corner of the past" on the Faubourg Saint-Honoré, between the Hermès store and the Rue Royale, had been the joy of a whole generation of collectors and enthusiasts. The public nature of a store window is something on which Maurice Segoura turned his back, preferring to arrange discreet meetings in his mansion, where clients could view his treasures. "My clients do not like to be seen through a store window. Here they are left in peace and the objects are placed in an appropriate setting." His clients are mainly financiers who do not have the time to hunt for antiques and prefer to put themselves into the hands of their dealer. "Times have changed. We used to learn a lot from our former clients, such as Arturo Lopez, who had plenty of leisure time. Today, our clients work and travel. Always on the go, they need a dealer they can trust, a place where they are comfortable and like to linger."

With its grand reception rooms and more intimate boudoirs, the Hôtel de Clermont-Tonnerre makes it possible to present various types of furniture, play with symmetry and combine items that have some affinity with their background. The large Boulle bureaux look well in the oak-paneled former dining room, the little marquetry tables and the china in the small round salons inspired by the Hôtel de Soubise, candlesticks and small cabinets in the long gallery, and everywhere paintings of various sizes which Maurice Segoura prefers to hang right on the paneled walls, like they would have been in old mansions. His love of the 18th century does not prevent him from making a few visits to the 19th century: a *Portrait of Marie d'Orléans* by Ary Scheffer, and a piece of imperial furniture, a gift from Napoleon, signed "Jacob Rue Meslée," "an exceptional piece of furniture, an art object, the beauty of bronzes"... The mansion, which still resounds to the Persian balls given by the Countess Blanche de Clermont-Tonnerre, has been brilliantly inaugurated by Maurice Segoura who intends, like Seligman in the Hôtel de Sagan, to make it a center for internationally renowned exhibitions.

SEGOURA
The corner drawing
room of the gallery.
On a marquetry and ormolu
table desk by Dubois, period of
Louis XV, a Louis XVI lyre clock.
Set of lacquered and gilt
wooden chairs signed by
Nadal Aîné, period of Louis XV.
The wing armchair near the
window is stamped I. Chevenat,
Louis XV period.
On the left, *La Danse dans un
pavillon* by Nicolas Lancret.

SEGOURA

Above: Chairs by Claude Séné, period Louis XV. A table desk stamped Jacques Dubois, period Louis XV with two China porcelain flowerpot holders, early 18th century. On the chest of drawers by Dubois, period Louis XV, a lyre clock, period Louis XVI. On the Regency period console, an obelisk clock, period Louis XVI. *Opposite:* In the dining room, *Portrait de Hyacinthe Sophie, marquise de Louville,* by H. Rigaud. Table in the center in ebony and ormolu by Joseph, Louis XVI period. Four gilt wooden armchairs, period Régence. Flat desk by Boulle, Louis XIV period. Savonnerie carpet.

BERNARD STEINITZ

Bernard Steinitz, 8ᵉ arr.

Can be described as: "hunter of objects." "I could not complete my education: it was the War, and I was on the run. I decided to work in this trade because I discovered the pleasures of the hunt, being in the midst of a crowd and seeing what others cannot see, something in an object that makes it different, rather special." Indeed, Bernard Steinitz is always on the lookout, always on the track of something, popping up where you least expect it, just like his hero Joseph Duveen. His omnipresence is very much in keeping with today's rapidly shifting international business climate. With his son Benjamin, he attends all the fairs and exhibitions, visits museums throughout the world, and keeps himself informed. Although he did not have the time to study much, his library, which contains numerous archives, could become, like that of Jacques Doucet, an enormous boon to researchers, scholars, and students.

"It's impossible for me to stay put and wait for clients to show up." He prefers to take a plane and buy in far-away places, visit his clients or his "children" sold to museums (about twenty items to the Metropolitan, twenty-five to the Getty). "An antique dealer today must be available three hundred and sixty-five days a year." Bernard Steinitz is self-taught and is grateful to those dealers who encouraged him to pursue his profession, such as Étienne Lévy to whom he showed a few objects and who replied very courteously: "They're not really what I'm looking for. But when you come to Paris, come and see me–I have an apartment devoted entirely to the 18th century." It is also through Lévy that he met René Weiller who impressed him with the speed of his judgement and whose catchphrase was: "In the time it takes for my colleagues to turn over an armchair and examine the base, I've already sold it twice."

After spending a little time on the Rue Rossini, Steinitz opened in the 1980s a showroom on the second floor of a building on the Rue Drouot which had been magnificently designed by the decorator Daniel Pasgrimaud; but he soon had his eye on the Faubourg Saint-Honoré, where he set up in a mansion in a courtyard. He can still be found in the neighborhood, in a modern gallery between the Avenue Matignon and the Rue du Cirque. This seasoned traveller is also very hospitable. He has a nostalgia for the grand turn-of-the-century interiors and paneling installed with brio by such great decorators as Barroux, Carlhian, and Jansen and has always strived to create interiors that are worthy of the objects and his clients. Even when short of space, as has been the case at certain Biennales, he always knew how to decorate with allusion, poetry and splendor, to offset his bronzes and lacquerware. "I have become my own decorator." This is a flair which he is able to share with those clients who have asked him to recreate French interiors for them. "The Germans want Louis XV and the Americans want Louis XVI, which goes better with their mahogany. We are currently installing some lovely paneling in Holland."

A sense of place, of welcome, a certain complicity. "I always take my clients to visit my restoration workshops so they can see what a piece of furniture looks like before it is restored." Leaning over the workbench, his eyes shining, Bernard Steinitz loves to speak tenderly of his concern for the relics of the past which are waiting for a new life. He also loves to take his clients to visit museums and Versailles. "We play the role of initiators, which is something the auction houses don't do." The 20th century is already turning into history. Like some of his clients, Bernard Steinitz is not insensitive to the talents of the great cabinet-makers of the 1920s, or the sumptuous decor of the Art Deco period… which retains the spirit of quality, craftsmanship and tradition. But, rest assured, "the 18th century remains the 18th century" and it still has a bright future ahead.

STEINITZ
Set of wooden panels decorated with French *chinoiseries* in black lacquer with red highlights in the taste of Jean Bérain, circa 1710-1720. In the foreground, a center table with ebony and bronze veneer, by Charles-Guillaume Winckelsen (1812-1871), with an ormolu ornamental freize in the taste of Delafosse (circa 1850). In the foreground, walnut armchair, Paris, circa 1740.

(following pages)
STEINITZ
Left: Main drawing room decorated with oak paneling, Regency period, installed at the beginning of the century by Georges Hoentschel in the town house of Sir Philip Sasson, 25 Park Lane, London. Set of one sofa and six gilt and painted wooden armchairs, Germany or Russia, early 19th century. Table desk of ebony and ormolu veneer, France, Regency period, circa 1730. *Right:* Hercules *fighting the centaur,* France, late 17th century, ormolu patina, by Ferdinando Tacca.

CHAPTER 3

JOUSSE-SEGUIN

Furniture by Jean Prouvé. A sun blind from the Tobacco factory of
Marseille, metal and aluminium sheet (1952). Mobile bracket-shaped lamp
(circa 1950). A wooden bowl by Alexandre Noll is set on a "compass table"
(sheet metal and laminated wooden top, *Cité internationale universitaire
of Paris,* 1950). Standard chairs (sheet metal and laminated wooden top).
On the right wall, writing case and shelf by Le Corbusier from the Franco-
Brazilian foundation of the *Cité internationale universitaire of Paris* (1956).

THE
MODERNS

ALEXANDRE BIAGGI

Alexandre Biaggi, 6ᵉ arr.

"We dreamed of periods that still seemed affordable to us and we tried to share our dream," says Alexandre Biaggi to summarize the story of his generation. Each period tends to look back with tenderness to the previous half century. The French Second Empire was nostalgic for the late 18th century; the Empress Eugenie fancied herself as Marie-Antoinette. Young people of the 1980s were attracted to the 1930s, leafing through back issues of *Vogue* and *Art et Industrie*. At the time, Charles de Beistegui, who lived in a modern apartment on the Champs-Élysées created by Le Corbusier, adorned it with button-upholstered furniture, baroque black-amoors, and Venetian mirrors, a mixture of austerity and folly, interpretations and almost surrealist displacements in time.

"I particularly liked the house designed by Louis Süe for Daisy Fellowes, with its grotto lined with stucco-framed mirrors and, of course, Jean-Michel Frank's great white living room for Charles and Marie-Laure de Noailles, for their home on the Place des États-Unis." For the children of post-modernism, the style between the two World Wars, with its follies and flights of fancy, had something of the Ancien Régime about it. "It was an era which displayed itself with a certain panache and nonchalance," as reproduced in the interiors by Christian Bérard or Jean Hugo for Jean-Michel Frank, of which Alexandre Biaggi is particularly fond.

After an apprenticeship with an auctioneer and diploma in hand, this antique dealer took off for the flea market, where he discovered the thirties. "Going from an office to owning a booth is to leave the world of business for the world of objects. What I enjoyed the most was discovering and buying." Sales were made to the great taste-makers of the day, Stéphane Deschamps, and the decorators Jean-Paul Faye and Jean-Louis Ricardi. When Biaggi started, you could still find Jean-Michel Frank pieces "for next to nothing," because "no one looked at it." Not only Frank, but Roche, Arbus, Moreux, and Poillerat. "This was called 'decoration furniture' as if all style is not decoration first and foremost. This kind of furniture has now become 'collection furniture' with a few more zeros added to the prices!"

Biaggi's move to the Left Bank marked the beginning of a new era. "It's much harder to express your taste in

BIAGGI
Three cerused oak chairs from a set of six, by Marc du Plantier, France, 1936.

BIAGGI

Opposite: On the wall a mirror console by Serge Roche (circa 1940) and two designs by Christian Bérard (circa 1940), white plaster standard-lamp by Jean-Michel Frank, specimen which used to be in the drawing room of the fashion house Lucien Lelong. One out of the pair patina and ormolu chandeliers with sixteen lights (France, late 1940s). Joseph Bernard : *Bacchante* of 1919, one of the three editions in plaster.

the flea market where there is a faster turnover. In a store, you have to do more: really relate to your choices, assert your taste in relation to the clientele and thus give the store a personality." Loving the 1930s also means including the painters who designed theatrical scenery, like Christian Bérard and Jean Hugo, as well as those who were called the "neo-romantics" because of their elegiac repertoire, such as Eugène Berman and his brother Léonide, as well as Pavel Tchelitcheff. Designs for furniture and the caprices of Emilio Terry, who also worked with Jean-Michel Frank, were the subject of a special exhibition in the *Salon de Mars.* "As in the 1930s, I would not hesitate to integrate a very beautiful 18th-century rock crystal chandelier or a handsome antique bust into the room decor." In fact, sculpture is Alexandre Biaggi's secret passion, from Clésinger to Joseph Bernard or Costi, who created the statues of the Groussay open-air theater. These larger-than-life figures currently dominate the gallery on the Rue de Seine.

CHRISTIAN BOUTONNET AND RAFAEL ORTIZ

L'Arc-en-Seine, 6ᵉ arr.

Christian Boutonnet emerged from the discreet charm of the 16th arrondissement, an apartment dominated by light-colored wood and opaline glass. He graduated from the select Janson de Sailly high school, then went on to become a dentist to please his family–which did not stop him from hunting down treasures of Art Deco, which he had learned to love during his student years, when he used to keep store for two friends for pocket money. Rafael Ortiz is from Barcelona, where he went to the Academy of Art, then worked in an architect's office where he traced drawings day in, day out, while spending his weekends hunting for antiques.

When the two collectors meet, they decide to shed their official jobs and open a small shop together in Les Halles area in 1977. They proceed to learn their trade by hunting through the flea market on the Rue des Rosiers, in a boutique near Paul Bert where a few Parisian dealers would come to look for stock. "Marc Lamouric, who sadly has passed away, did much to guide us in our choices. There were large portraits by Yakovlev, decorative reliefs from the 1937 Exposition, and Pierre Legrain's African-inspired works. He reacted immediately and enabled us to benefit from his intuition. He's the one who encouraged us to take the giant step."

Preceded by two other colleagues from Les Halles (Maria de Beyrie and the Vallois couple), they moved to the Rue de Seine–where their gallery became L'Arc-en-Seine–and began to assert their style. "From the outset, we wanted to distance ourselves from classic Art Deco, to forget Ruhlmann, Süe and Mare and Leleu to discover the innovators of the period."

Their first enthusiasm was for the work of Pierre Chareau, whose glass house is an example of successful modernism in their opinion and whose modular furniture, combining wood and iron, craftsmanship and futurism, luxury and apparent simplicity enchant them. They also like humorous pieces as witnessed by *La Grande Religieuse,* one of their cult objects. They organized the first Chareau exhibition a year before his work was shown at the Pompidou Center, after which his fame spread beyond the circle of initiates. This was followed by a presentation of furnishings in walnut and sycamore designed by Robert Mallet-Stevens for Villa Cavroix. One of the satisfactions of the dealer is contributing to help people and things to find each other. "We sold this furniture to a collector who had just moved into the apartment of the Martel brothers' town house, which had actually been designed by Mallet-Stevens."

Conscious of their role as discoverers of a century, they want the works to be appreciated by a wider public and have organized several memorable exhibitions. The Edward James Foundation called them in to display the

(following pages)
BOUTONNET ET ORTIZ
Left: On a parchment and oak console table by Paul Dupré-Lafon (circa 1935), a walnut lamp, an inkstand and a paperweight by Jean-Michel Frank (circa 1930). The two bronze dogs are by Diego Giacometti (circa 1970). On the wall, a gouache by Christian Bérard, *Les As du tapis* (1930). In the foreground, two leather armchairs by Paul Dupré-Lafon (circa 1930). *Right:* On a Macassar ebony table by Jacques-Émile Ruhlmann (circa 1928), a pair of hammered pewter vases (1925), a head of a woman in ormolu by Alberto Giacometti (circa 1930). Above the sketch of Christian Bérard an alabaster and silverbronze wall lamp (circa 1925).

work of Alberto Giacometti which had been acquired in the 1930s and 1950s by this famous collector and patron of the Surrealists. This was followed by an exhibition devoted entirely to the "bestiary" of his brother Diego. In a show revolving around Jean-Michel Frank, they exhibited the set he created for the theater director Raymond Rouleau as well as work by Frank's admired collaborators, including Christian Bérard's rare watercolors of interiors and Emilio Terry's rocaille consoles which, according to the press, redefined popular notions of 20th-century style and taste.

At the 1992 Biennale, they exhibited work by Printz, Dunand, and Cheuret, a screen by Dunand and lamps by Giacometti, but the highlight of the display was undoubtedly a table by Lalique. Alerted by the press, visitors stood in line to marvel at it under the neo-classical arches of Pier Luigi Pizzi. All this homage to their favorite century does not prevent them from promoting contemporary arts and crafts, such as the work of the master glassblower Laura de Santillana, whose talents were revealed in France for the first time in 2000.

ANTOINE BROCCARDO

Alb Antiquités, 7ᵉ arr.

His native town is Nice, but he is of Corsican and Italian extraction. He attended a technical high school, learned ceramics with his teacher Lebasque (the painter's grandson). Later, at the age of sixteen, Antoine Broccardo started a school of decorative arts and was introduced to metal work. He was highly influenced by a childhood friend who wrote a thesis entitled *Aesthetics of the throne, tiara, sepulchre and poison,* which was devoted to decorative arts at the end of the century. Together they discovered Symbolism and Art Nouveau. They made a pilgrimage to the Chéret Museum, to see the work of Gustave Mossa which no one was interested in at the time, and they haunted the *bric-à-brac* shops, searching for Art Nouveau ceramics, lamps, small pieces of furniture. Their favorite books: *Aesthetes and Magicians* by Philippe Jullian and *The Style of Jules Verne* by Maurice Rheims. Then Antoine Broccardo quit his studies to learn the job of window-dresser. In 1974, he went to Paris where he worked for Charles Jourdan and discovered Carlo Bugatti, Eileen Grey, and Marcel Coard.

Antoine Broccardo got hooked and went on hunting at the bookstalls along the Seine for data from this period. The 50th Jubilee Exhibition of the Decorative Arts, which took place at the Decorative Arts Museum, fired his enthusiasm. He discovered a spirit, a new aesthetic, always specialized in ceramic, metal and glasswork. Simultaneously, he discovered sculpture with Frémiet and Stuck, Janine Janet and Gérôme, as well as neo-Greek and Japanese-style objects through a casket by Diehl, metalwork by Reiber, ceramics by Deck. He had the taste of the great in small artefacts. He progressed from his humble beginnings in a 6 square-meter booth at Palais-Royal, to a 12-meter-long corridor on Rue du Bouloi, then the 20 square meters of the shop *Alb Antiquités* on Rue Allent, before establishing "between street and garden," in the Rue de Lille in 1998.

Upon entering this modern cabinet of curiosities, you will discover an Art Deco bust by Rex Ingram and a small bronze by George Minne, a candlestick by Gustave Serrurier-Bovy and an enameled mirror by Emilio Terry. All the techniques of that inventive period are welcome here—gold and jewelry, sheet metal, iridescent blown glass, lacquerware and ceramics, because the only thing that counts is the quality of the material and the skill of the craftsman. Antoine Broccardo's original calling as a window-dresser gave him a feel for what goes with what and what contrasts with what, and he is a man of boundless curiosity. Darmstadt, Munich, Glasgow, Berlin, Vienna, and Brussels are for him capitals of good taste just as much as Paris. He pioneered the discovery of German rococo and the intimate theater of Dagobert Peche, as well as the paintings of great decorators

ANTOINE BROCCARDO
On the sculptor's pedestal, bronze head of *Actéon,* unique specimen by Janine Janet. Above, an articulated iron and brass dummy of the 19th century. On the green lacquered console by Bruno Paul, circa 1920, two fô dogs in German porcelain by Gustav Oppel, 1925. The tortoiseshell and gilt wood mirror is by Gustav Franck. A pair of frosted glass chandeliers by Süe and Mare, 1925. Cubic armchair, out of a pair, by Paul Poiret (ateliers Martine), 1914.

such as Yakovlev and the ceramics of Georges Hugnet. He may be an expert in German and Austrian Jugendstil and British Liberty style, but he can also discern in French Art Nouveau the austere lines which link it to the Arts and Crafts movement or the follies which heralded the advent of Surrealism. He has held various exhibitions in his different galleries. His neo-Russian furniture is one of the most unexpected discoveries of Art Nouveau; his "masks" and "boxes" are full of mystery and imagination.

ALINE CHASTEL AND LAURENT MARÉCHAL
Galerie Chastel-Maréchal, 6ᵉ arr.

"When I wanted to write my master's thesis in the late 1980s on the subject of Carabin, the name was quite unknown to anyone at the university," Aline Chastel explains. She subsequently studied at the Icart school which prepares students for "artistic occupations." There she met Laurent Maréchal who, after difficult exams at the landscaping school in Versailles, was thinking of switching to antiques. "I had always been something of an antique hound. I remember the large Thonet chair which was square in cross-section, used to prop up a wash-basin in the equivalent of a Salvation Army store. I had to bargain for it, I was 15 years old at the time." At the Icart school, Roger-Henri Guerrand, the author of a history of water closets, instilled the love of 20th century artefacts, though the ground had already been well prepared. "We were more interested in Pop Art than in a Louis XV cabriolet or soft paste porcelain." Laurent and Alice graduate the same year and started working in the flea market in 1990.

"It was enjoyable dealing in small items, Jourdain ceramics, a leather Adnet, Lalique flasks, whatever happened along… We dealt in just about everything while we were learning the trade. Then we latched onto the 1940s as an antidote to Art Deco, with spectacular, gilded extravaganzas, a sort of Napoleon III button upholstery. People made fun of us." Consulting documentation of the period enabled them to sort out the good from the bad and put names to pieces, including the Giacometti brothers, Quinet, Moreux, Poillerat, and Roche, which they sold to the dealers in the Palais-Royal or on the Rue Bonaparte. "A large mirror-covered table by Serge Roche only stayed three quarters of an hour after it had been unpacked at the Puces." Many of the items pictured in the book entitled *Décorateurs des années quarante* (Decorators of the 1940s) passed through their hands. "At the time, we were selling to Yves Gastou and Éric Philippe, but the pioneer was and remains Anne-Sophie Duval, who had 1940s artefacts in her showroom before anyone else." And then there was a desire to make their mark, to make deliberate choices, and to defend a certain type of merchandise.

"Yves Gastou told us that lots of stores were empty on the Rue Bonaparte. This was in November 1994, during the Recession, so nobody encouraged us to take the risk. But we opened up at number 10, between Gastou and Marcilhac." American decorators such as Jed Johnson and Robert Couturier found their way to the tiny gallery and discovered André Arbus, Gilbert Poillerat, Maxime Old, René Prou, and Jean Royère. "In a gallery, there is a different way of discovering and studying an object. You have the time to prepare a group of objects for an exhibition, such as a set of mirrors and bronzes by Line Vautrin." A move across the street from 10 to 5 marked the rise of Aline Chastel and Laurent Maréchal. Important clients, like important objects, need space in which to spread out and look their best. But life goes on, and now they are into the 1960s. To be continued…

STÉPHANE DESCHAMPS

Stéphane Deschamps, 6ᵉ arr.

To his embarrassment, all the young dealers of today consider Deschamps to be the ultimate authority on everything that is 1930s and 1940s, the person who has seen everything, who spotted everything before anyone else did and who will continue to surprise everyone.

He is the person who had and continues to have all the biggest clients, the legendary collectors. Protesting modesty, Stéphane Deschamps hides behind his success. He has always remained faithful to the Rue Guénégaud "where the grass used to grow" when he first arrived.

He wanted to be an actor. He likes to recall his performances in plays which, if he is to be believed, were all spectacular flops. But the interpreter of minor marquis or of Perdican was beset by doubts: "You have no talent, you love beautiful things, you stop." A painter friend, Édouard MacAvoy, and an antique dealer friend sent him to the Village Suisse (antique district in the 15th *arrondissement*) to see Bernadette Fenwick, granddaughter of Jacques Rouché, administrator of the Ballets Russes and the Paris Opéra. Fenwick was one of the first dealers in Art Nouveau. "The store was called *Sirius*. I saw a lady standing on a stepladder who was knocking in nails and who said to me, 'Pass me the hammer.' I passed her the hammer and two minutes later, she said to me: 'Well, what do you want?' I replied, 'Madame, I would like to work with antiques, I have been sent by…' 'I warn you,' she told me, 'we'll only have time to go to the swimming pool three times a week. Here, pass me that and that.' And that's how I began."

Saint Laurent, Pierre Bergé, and Pierre Cardin dropped in every Sunday. Then, after a delightful interlude in Saint-Tropez, where Stéphane Deschamps sold painted Bavarian closets and decorative items—"It was an extraordinary life, we spent every day on the beach. We lunched with Jean-Marie Rivière, opened up at five in the afternoon and went out every evening." His father put a stop to this idle life. "Now you have to work, I'll buy you a store." "I opened with Majorelle furniture, a mantelpiece by Müller, bronzes by Bugatti, and lamps by Gallé. Karl Lagerfeld, Saint Laurent, and Hélène Rochas came to the store the very next day. At that time, Léonor Fini bought a roomful of furniture and Liz Taylor collected Lalique and *pâte de verre*."

This full-blooded entry into Art Nouveau did not prevent Stéphane Deschamps from keeping a weakness for the 19th century. "I am from a bourgeois provincial family. 19th-century houses are easy to furnish while to be able to afford Art Deco, you have to be one of the knights of industry." This atavism enabled him to rediscover the furniture of Fourdinois and Jeanselme long before it was exhibited at the Orsay Museum. He also loved the sculptures of Dalou, Maindron, and Carpeaux, ranging from busts of the imperial family to small animals. "It was an astonishing period, where you could buy in junk markets huge pieces by Barye and where Decamps'were lying on the ground."

Philippe Jullian and André Ciechanowiecki encouraged him to pursue this avenue but he was also attracted by the 1920s and 1930s. "I think I was one of the first to discover Jean-Michel Frank, in the late 1960s. I saw the first ones at Marie-Laure de Noailles. Of course, I also had some Ruhlmann, some Dunand, just like everyone else, but I think that you just have to let yourself go. I have always loved kitsch." Although he is capable of finding plain Art Deco items for the austere clientele of the decorator Serge Royaux, he also loves to explore the world of fantasy as in the plasterwork and mirrors of Serge Roche or the rope furniture of Audoux-Minet, and even slightly Surrealist objects, such as the glove in silvered bronze which he sold to Visconti. "I even sold something to Dali, when he was keen on Amanda Lear. It was one of the most kitsch lamps I ever had, in the form of a porcelain Colombine, whose skirt was the lampshade. I also sold some Chiparus pieces to Franco Maria

DESCHAMPS
In front of a 17th-century painted canvas, two big ceramic vases by Jacques Lenoble and a ceramic vase by Jean Besnard. They are standing on an oak and Madagascar hemp table by Audoux-Minet.

DESCHAMPS

Above: Symbolist colored marble and bronze female bust. Plaster head of a woman by Osouf, terra cotta relief by Gilbert Privat.
Silver tray, 1900. Two ceramics by Herbst, *Lapithe et centaure* by Barye, cast-iron by the artist, numbered.
Opposite: On an easel, a cat by Koyanagui (Paris, 1930s) On the plaster console by Serge Roche, two gilt cardboard
and plaster masks, 1930, attributed to Messel. On the wall, an *Allegory of Architecture,* terra cotta-colored plaster,
attributed to Androusoff. Above a gilt wooden sofa, stamped Jeanselme, hangs a still life with orchids (Russia, 1950s).

Ricci, but which rather upset me, because I thought they were abominable." Deschamps is inquisitive and not blinded by preconceived notions. He has a weakness for the paintings of the realists of the 1930s, such as Ismael de la Serna and for neo-romanticists like Bérard, Berman, and Tchelitchev. But he is always happy to find a canvas by his friend, MacAvoy.

Those who frequent the Rue Guénégaud are very familiar with Stéphane Deschamps' storage room in the courtyard. That's where, after seating you comfortably in one of the deep sofas, he'll push aside the screens and show you his "unsellable stuff"—reliefs by the Martel brothers, souvenirs of the 1937 Fair—which, never fear, will find their place sooner or later in some American museum.

JEAN-JACQUES DUTKO

Galerie Jean-Jacques Dutko, 6ᵉ arr.

Take an inherited booth at the Marché aux Puces, and an antique dealer friend in the provinces who supplied him with merchandise on a regular basis… and the situation is almost irresistible. For several years, Jean-Jacques Dutko served his apprenticeship at Vernaison flea market, subsequently starting a booth at which he sold quality 18th-century furniture. He opened a branch at the Village Suisse. Then there was a new development: a doctor friend of his showed him an amazing desk he had just bought. "It's Art Deco, a Pierre Chareau," he explained. It was back in the early 1970s; Jean-Jacques Dutko started research, visited the architect's Glass House and decided to build up a stock of Art Deco. He set up shop amid the pioneers of the district Anne-Sophie Duval and Félix Marcilhac, at 5, Rue Bonaparte.

"I've always loved architect-designed furniture. Pierre Chareau was the trigger, then I discovered Ruhlmann, Dupré-Lafon, Printz, a whole tradition of well-designed furniture with clean lines, using metal and lacquer. I love Ruhlmann when he is very inventive." Meeting Guy Bujon, a collector and devotee of Eugène Printz, caused him to embark on a publishing venture. Together they traced the work of the artist through his former clients and published a monograph on the pieces they had managed to bring to light. The Dutko gallery devoted an entire exhibition to Printz, the first of his work.

The first time Dutko participated in the 1982 Biennale, he displayed lacquered furniture by Eugène Printz, Jean Dunand, and Pierre Chareau. His customers shared his love of modern art and he decided that he would display it in his new gallery, decorated by Jean-Michel Wilmote, on the corner of the Rue des Beaux-Arts and the Rue Bonaparte. He also exhibited at the *Salon de Mars* where he displayed modern classics, contemporary artists and items of Art Deco furniture. The combination was a success and it caused him to ask plastic artists such as Bruno Romeda, Jean-Pierre Pincemin, and Jean-Paul Reti, to create furniture just for him. The "Dutko style" which he exhibits in his own apartment—a triple adventure in esthetics combining contemporary art, Art Deco furniture and African sculpture—has seduced some of his clients into becoming more daring. It is a successful formula which he regularly repeats during the temporary exhibitions at the gallery, when he displays his latest finds.

DUTKO
In the foreground, close-up of the lacquered seat by Katsu Hamanaka and a carpet by Léon Jallot. On the glass and bronze table by Bruno Romeda, an Atie statue from the Ivory Coast. In the background, the lacquered screen by Jean Dunand is standing in front of a sculpture, *Cerchio,* by Bruno Romeda. On the right, a jar gilded in gold leaf by Jean-Pierre Raynaud.

ANNE-SOPHIE DUVAL

Anne-Sophie Duval, 6ᵉ arr.

Anne-Sophie Duval was born into the trade and her progression illustrates the development of the market for 20th century items. Her mother, Yvette Barran, was a pioneer in Art Nouveau in the late 1950s. Maurice Rheims sent her a few clients and all the antique-hunters would share the address "of that crazy woman on the Rue Bonaparte who sells retro items."

"We lived over the store. The atmosphere was very convivial, very "Saint-Germain-des-Prés." The kitchen, which had a little bar, was just in the back of the shop. The first customers included Marie-Laure de Noailles, Nourhan Manoukian, Pierre Bergé, Yves Saint Laurent, and Agnelli. The curators of the big German museums also came once a week to do their shopping. I myself used to hunt for antiques at the Marché aux Puces every Saturday. Then, around 1965, Art Deco suddenly took off. We learned a lot from the children of the artists who would tell us about 'Dad.' Madame Printz sold us the furniture belonging to her husband which had remained behind in the store on the Faubourg Saint-Honoré, from which she still worked as a decorator. Some apartments were still intact, such as Marcel L'Herbier's, with its set of Chareau furniture, but I did not understand everything. I remember going, when I was twenty, to Boulogne to see Marc du Plantier, but I found his work too abstract, too empty." It was also the era of the real estate boom which endangered the small town houses in the 16th arrondissement. "Often I would arrive at these magnificent empty houses: you could see the marks of the paintings where they used to be on the walls, and a few pieces of "retro junk" would be shoved into a corner. For the owners, who were only interested in keeping their oldest furniture, it would either go to us or the demolishers. Sometimes, I got there too late."

The year 1972 was a memorable one. Anne-Sophie took over *Carmontel,* an old-fashioned place which sold 18th-century antiques, and exhibited at her first Biennale. The stand designed by Karl Lagerfeld had glossy green walls and a floor in black rubber. On display were pieces of furniture, vases and a screen by Jean Dunand, as well as a lacquered table by Pierre Legrain. A Fernand Léger lent by the Galerie Leiris adorned the wall.

Anne-Sophie Duval's favorites include Paul Iribe and Armand-Albert Rateau, whose famous bronze *chaise longue* and armchair with fish she discovered, and she has a special preference for Pierre Chareau: "He is the best of the best: inventive Art Deco, architectural furniture for an intellectual clientele, so different from Ruhlmann. This was at a time when Frank did not yet exist commercially. When we found pieces by him, we kept them for ourselves."

Her move into the 1940s was a natural progression. She made the transition smoothly, discovering along the way a few exceptional pieces which initiated her into the new decade. "What interests me most is the way volumes are dealt with–the materials are less important. People made fun of one of my first purchases, a neo-rococo console table by Jean-Charles Moreux; today, it is in a major collection in New York." Then came Paul Dupré-Lafon, André Arbus, Jacques Adnet. Her predilection for ceramics led her to discover the Art Nouveau ceramicists, then the work of designers such as Jean Desprès.

Despite a memorable Rateau exhibition organized with the help of the artist's family and several collectors, and a brilliant display at the Biennale, Anne-Sophie Duval prefers to concentrate on dealing, in her gallery which– now that certain objects sold in those pioneering years have come back to the store–has become once again a must for lovers of the first half of the 20th century.

DUVAL
On a console with terra cotta table-top and wrought-iron feet by Jean-Charles Moreux (circa 1938), a ceramic vase by Jean Besnard. Mirror with fishskin frame by André Groult.

DUVAL

Above: Details of three chairs: Eileen Gray, oak armchair in the Arts and
Crafts style, circa 1910. Jean-Michel Frank, a pair of oak chairs, circa 1935.
Ernest Boiceau, X-framed stool, light mahogany covered with "point Cornely"
material, circa 1935. *Opposite:* On three black lacquered nesting tables, two
porcelain jars with lids by Maurice Gensoli, circa 1940.

YVES GASTOU

Galerie Yves Gastou, 6ᵉ arr.

"It is not an occupation, it's a vocation," claims Yves Gastou, who doesn't need to be asked twice to revive his "prim-ordial scene": the loss of a present from his mother, a little bronze cannon, which led him to hunt for antiques. He was helped in his quest by his father, a court bailiff who, on certain Sundays, served as an auctioneer in the mar-ket hall of Limoux. While rummaging through the baskets, the child found crosses, medals, old photographs, and engravings. On Thursday afternoons, his mother would take him for walks in Carcassonne where a few old ladies dressed in black, the "antiquaries," reigned over the mysterious empire of the past: "kings, lords, princes." The pomp and ceremony of the Catholic church did little to assuage Gastou's desire for splendor: "I stood in line seve-ral times to kiss the rings of the bishop, who sat under a canopy of ostrich feathers, surrounded by the odor of incense." His school record was disastrous so, when he was 16, his sensible mother sent him to become the appren-tice of "Monsieur Thomas, antique dealer," a furniture remover specializing in hospices, vicarages, and castles. But the local market was disappointing–the best pieces went to Paris. "A Louis XV chest of drawers or a Louis-Philippe secretary did not excite me. When you begin in this trade, you need to be unconventional, provocative."

In his first little store in Carcassonne, Gastou stocked Gallé furniture, small turn-of-the-century sculptures, a few items of glass. He had a local customer base and also supplied the Paris trade by looking for items from country homes between Nice and Biarritz. Gradually, he expanded to Jacques-Émile Ruhlmann, Pierre Chareau, Armand-Albert Rateau, Eileen Gray, and Pierre Legrain. But perhaps those names were too familiar already and he wanted to cause a stir... He moved to Toulouse in 1972 with his wife Françoise, who left the legal profession to join the antiques business. In 1978, he exhibited an "anonymous living room set, the height of kitsch." He discovered Poillerat, then Arbus who hailed from Toulouse, and Adnet. In an unexpected way, he was returning to the childhood dreams of castles, princes, and kings. "These designers never made a clean sweep of the past. Whether they're austere, kitch or totally mind-blowing, you can always recognize a traditional reference–baroque or neo-classical–although I do also appreciate the austere phase some of them went through." Across the street from Yves and Françoise was a modern gallery that sold Knoll, Cassina, and Memphis. "It was love at first sight for contemporary works. I learned to look at everything differently." They sold objects designed by Raymond Loewy, Sottsas prototypes, as well as 1950s Murano glass, Carlo Mollino and Gio Ponti furniture." They decided to move to Paris.

After a brief stint at the Marché aux Puces, they moved to the Rue Bonaparte in 1984, where they commissioned Sottsass to design the display window, an affirmation of their contemporary approach to the 20th century. The work of Ettore Sottsas, as well as that of André Dubreuil, Ron Arad, Tom Dixon, Shiro Kuramata, and Garouste and Bonetti was featured. As a counterpoint, they paid tribute to "great artists who, as early as 1968, were considered outcasts:" first and foremost Gilbert Poillerat, as well as André Arbus, Marc du Plantier, Jean Pascaud, Jean-Charles Moreux, and Maxime Old. These exhibitions are sometimes accompanied by group catalogs or monographs which bear the hallmark of Gastou and reflect his way of looking at things. The exhibition entitled *Décorateurs des années quarante* which he directed at the Boulogne-Billancourt Cultural Center in the winter of 1998, was the culmination of his work as a pioneer, from which the Biennale had already largely benefitted. Gastou "traditions" include figurative sculpture of the 1930s, with such names of Alfred Janniot, Charles Despiau, Hubert Yencesse, Vadim Androusov, André Arbus, and later Robert Couturier. A tradition that is still alive, since the photographer Marie-Pierre Decuyper was invited to exhibit her "sculptural nudes" in the gallery on the Rue Bonaparte.

GASTOU
Tapestry *Le jour et la nuit* by Picart Ledoux. In the corner, *Actéon,* a bronze by André Arbus. On the short-piled Aubusson car-pet by Jacques Quinet, a pedestal table by André Arbus, with a bronze by Henry Parayre. A pair of blackened pear and black leather armchairs by André Arbus, with ormolu arm-rests by Androusoff. Monumental wrought-iron chandelier by Gilbert Poillerat.

GASTOU

Above: Jacques Adnet, desk covered with original chestnut-brown leather and matching chair (1950).
Stone *Minerva,* 1940s. *Opposite:* Wrought-iron day-bed, gilded in its entirety in gold leaf by André Arbus,
in front of a wooden three-panel screen, showing Trojan knights, signed V.P. Cayeux, 1950.
Wrought-iron pedestal table and lamp by Gilbert Poillerat.

PHILIPPE JOUSSE AND PATRICK SEGUIN

Galerie Jousse-Seguin, 11ᵉ arr.

The notable arrival of Philippe Jousse and Patrick Seguin on the scene of the last Biennale of the 20th century marked the entry of that century into history. Two steps from the delightful 18th century paneling in *vernis Martin* where *bonheurs-du-jour* with elaborate flower marquetry were displayed, the bare floor and plasterboard partitions of the Jousse-Seguin Gallery, streaked with the blue powder of the masons, was a fitting backdrop to the pure forms in plywood, tubes or molded sheet-iron of Jean Prouvé, Jean Royère, Charlotte Perriand, and Le Corbusier. Called into question in the 1980s by the insolent wave of post-modernism, the great modernists got their revenge by insinuating themselves discreetly into the antiques market.

Jean Prouvé stood out amongst them. "He was a trigger for me, yet I hadn't even heard of him. I knew of Le Corbusier and, at the time, I would tiptoe into the *Mobilier International* store. What I liked in his case was this combination of a craftsman's approach and industrial technology, this honesty of constructed form, this intransigeance, this parallelism between architecture and design. For me, he represents a major synthesis in the 20th century," explains Philippe Jousse. Yet ideas and concepts were not what Jousse's business was about in Vanves and at Paul-Bert in 1980: he was selling objects–objects with a past which, through their well-worn and scuff-marked existence, brought with them a slice of history reflecting the industrial and collective utopias of the century. "We are sometimes confronted with difficult problems in restoration–whether we should try to restore the object to how it originally looked or include the traces of subsequent usage," explains Patrick Séguin, who usually prefers to leave the marks. This respectful attitude enables examples of industrial archeology to enter the esthetic sphere of collectors of primitive or contemporary art.

The partnership with Patrick Seguin in first one, then two galleries in the Bastille district confirmed this connection to the plastic arts. Furniture, objects, and contemporary works were presented alternately or simultaneously. Their regular participation in the international contemporary art fairs held in Basel, Berlin, and Chicago confirmed this osmosis which was obvious in the Jean Prouvé exhibition in 1994, in which the artist's table legs were displayed like sculpture and the *Pièces-Meublés* exhibit in 1995, in which Rudolf Stingel, Thomas Grünfeld, and Bertrand Lavier integrated Prouvé creations into their own work. This impressive task of rediscovery culminated in another exhibition in 1998 in collaboration with the Enrico Navarra Gallery. The white walls of the gallery on the Rue de Charonne highlight the structure of the furniture and prefabricated houses designed by Prouvé. They had been displayed by Philippe Jousse and Patrick Seguin at the previous Venice Architecture Biennale, the last joint venture of the partners who have decided to split up and go their separate ways.

JOUSSE-SEGUIN
In the spacy gallery of the Rue des Taillandiers, a set of furniture by Jean Prouvé: bed *Flavigny* (circa 1950), desk (1950), secretary-desk (circa 1950), table *Granito* (circa 1950), mobile bracket lamp (circa 1950) and, on the wall in the background, sun blinds (1952). The lamp is by Serge Mouille, the LCW (Long Chair Wood) is by Charles Eames (circa 1945).

JACQUES LACOSTE

Galerie Jacques Lacoste, 7ᵉ arr.

After studying Art History and Law at the University of Nanterre, with further training at the Icart School, Jacques Lacoste learned the trade during an internship with an auctioneer. A structured job in the traditional firm of Couturier-Nicolay, with its refined client contacts, discreet sales of inheritance and classic deals. The very antithesis of the Marché aux Puces, where he had a booth from 1986 to 1990, a brutal and rapid apprenticeship to the trade. "It was a condensed version of all the dirty tricks, bad purchases made at 5 A.M., having

to stay vigilant and on the lookout, merchandise that comes and goes and, most of all, the obligation to buy anything that looks interesting, without really having much choice."

It was a time when he made some great finds: a surprising set of furniture by Eugène Gaillard, a long seat by Giacometti. And when he learned from the customers, collectors, and other dealers. These included certain pioneers, such as Philippe Jousse, François Laffanour, and Alan, who introduced Lacoste to the 1950s styles. Alan, who operated from the Rue de Lille, had a Serge Mouille exhibition in 1982-1983. It was through Alan that Lacoste discovered an artist who was to become his passion–Jean Royère, "an example of creativity without restraints, funny, playful and casual." Lacoste contacted those who had launched this artist before him, such as Axel de Heeckeren and Pierre Passebon, and learned as much as he could. "When you discover an artist, you need to be able to get the research done, read everything that has been published and, above all, get an idea of his development. Royère, who is always considered an artist of the 1950s, had actually invented everything before the War."

His move to the Rue de Lille in 1997 gave him the chance to defend his choices and give the showroom a certain style, specializing in the second half of the 20th century. The purchase of voluminous Royere archives enabled Lacoste to discover the scope of the artist's output, the range of his commissions, and to make contacts with former clients and the Royère family. An exhibition in 1998, for which a catalog was prepared, set the values and caused the Decorative Arts Museum to present its own Royère material. The market has developed rapidly. Former barriers collapsed, the separation still in existence in the 1980s between "pioneers" and "traditionalists," between the *Union des Artistes Modernes* (UAM, Union of Modern Artists) and the *Société des Artistes Décorateurs* (SAD, Decorative Artists Society) no longer made any sense. "The same collectors are buying Prouvé, Royère, and Charlotte Perriand which they would match with a Brancusi or a Picasso. The 1930s, 1950s, 1970s, and contemporary art look fine together in minimalist surroundings." While American clients, often accompanied by their decorators (Thierry Desponds, Allan Wanzenberg) still keep coming, a new French customer base is emerging, and there is growing interest from institutions such as the Vitra Museum and MoMA. Jacques Lacoste likes outsiders. In addition to Royère, he promotes Alexandre Noll, an artist who carves crude furniture and pure forms out of the hardest woods. This universality of the plastic arts is something which attracts him, as illustrated by an aluminum sculpture which is actually a prototype for a Serge Mouille lamp.

LACOSTE
Two seats *Œuf* armchairs by Jean Royère, chair by Alexandre Noll (1947), floor lamp with three arms by Serge Mouille.

FRANÇOIS LAFFANOUR

Galerie Down Town, 6ᵉ arr.

"I studied history in the years after the 1968 upheaval, and there was nothing on the surface to predispose me for this occupation. Neither was I planning on becoming a teacher," admits François Laffanour. At the time, the "humanities" were still considered solid training and history, like philosophy, was the gateway to anything. A road accident left him with compensation which he invested in a shop at the flea market and rented to a dealer in rustic furniture. "I wanted him to take me as a salesman, but it didn't work out because I was already interested in the 20th century."

Encountering Jean Prouvé was fateful, as Prouvé's aspirations satisfied the demands of the intellectual Laffanour. "His work is the extreme opposite of decoration. It was a very non-conformist thing to do, putting office and industrial furniture into the home. This belief in new materials, new technologies, this desire to bring them to the masses could only please me as a historian.

(following pages)
LAFFANOUR
Left: Bookcase by Charlotte Perriand and Jean Prouvé, private commission, 1952. Carlo Mollino, chair made for the *Lutrario Dance Hall* in Torino in 1959. Jean Prouvé, table *Granito,* 1945. *Right:* George Nelson, sofa *Marshmallow,* produced since 1956.

Prouvé's choice of humble materials—sheet metal and plywood, for instance—made it possible to appreciate shape for its own sake, but the constructive design eliminated formalistic complacencies." These multiple discrepancies between the original intentions and the resulting object, the industrial product and its reappropriation through time and history satisfied both the theoretician and the esthete which Laffanour is, despite his protestations to the contrary.

Thanks to the collectors and dealers of his generation, the 20th century with its industrial and colonial utopias, its collectivist generosities and desire for eternity, enters history. François Laffanour speaks of the patina on his painted sheets of metal with more lyricism than many 18th-century specialists do about their wooden carvings. For Laffanour there is nothing more moving than a sheet of painted iron that has seen better times; each groove, each scratch, each graze domesticates an industrial object, gives it a personality, transforms it into the memory of an existence or a plan. Its patina humanizes the industrial drawing. With Prouvé, the craftsman is always close to the designer and his "coquetry" has its humour.

In the same vein is Charlotte Perriand, whose free forms and love of wood have contributed to the livening of the austere spaces of modern architecture. "I love the mixture of sobriety and subtlety, such as in the Villa Savoye, for example." His other protégés include Charles Eames, whose home-handyman simplicity he finds moving.

After staying at the Marché aux Puces until the late 1970s, Laffanour founded the first 1950s gallery (in the world) on the Rue de Provence, near the Drouot auction rooms. In 1980, he moved on to the Rue de Seine, working with Mara Cremniter, a pioneer in modern and contemporary glassware. Then came the decorators and American clients who made Prouvé into a new star whom the fashion industry and showbiz have appropriated. Does this threaten the non-conformism of the rediscovery? François Laffanour sees the emergence of new strata of clients, who are younger and more inquisitive, through the eyes of whom it will be possible to discover different aspects of a period that is really too close to be truly assimilated. "Le Corbusier himself is far from being well known, as far as furnishings are concerned. He has a lot to teach us about the relationship between the object and its architectural environment."

FÉLIX MARCILHAC

Félix Marcilhac, 6e arr.

"When you can afford to buy a Brancusi, you'll see, you'll give it all up," a collector once told Félix Marcilhac in the 1960s. He had just made his first purchase, a Miklos bronze. "I have hated that man all my life for saying that: no one has the right to say that to an enthusiastic kid of 23." As so often happens, the enthusiasm began by accident.

"I am of modest origins: my parents were small shopkeepers. I got a bachelor's degree in Economics and studied at the *École Supérieure de Sciences Politiques,* then I worked for two years in the movie industry. From the movies to set decoration, set decoration to antiques, I discovered the flea market and made my first forays there. I used to shop there on Friday and Saturday mornings, reselling the same items in Saint-Germain on the same afternoon to Jeanne Fillon, *Comoglio* or Yvette Barant, or to Bernadette Fenwick at the Village Suisse."

"In the early 1960s, Art Nouveau, which was referred to as 'noodle' style, was just being rediscovered and nothing at all was known about Art Deco, whose artefacts were referred to as 'retro.' There was a very depre-

MARCILHAC
Jacques-Emile Ruhlmann, armchair, 1925. On the wall, preliminary full-size sketch for a carpet, made for Jacques Doucet by Gustave Miklos. *Arbre cubiste* by Joël and Jan Martel, 1925.

catory connotation of something outlandish, furniture for the crazy, which was used mainly for decorating period movies or for furnishing the apartments of rather exuberant people." At the Sorbonne, Marcilhac discovered Cubism with Jean Laude and wrote an Master's thesis on the Martel brothers, then launched into a doctoral thesis on Csaky, which he hopes to finish one day. His mentors included Stéphane Deschamps: "I would trot around the flea market after him and watch him buy Gallé vases which I thought were hideous–which I ended up loving once I understood them–, but I was fascinated by what he had to say."

He opened his store on the Rue Bonaparte in 1969, selling Art Nouveau and pitch pine, steel or cast iron furniture, as well as some contemporary furniture purchased at the Milan Triennial. In 1970, he found himself alone at the helm. He gradually began to discover Art Deco, trailing his favorite artists. Other pioneers followed in his footsteps. "Maurice Rheims would come in to discuss the price of a floor lamp by Brandt, Hélène Rochas was combining Art Deco with the 18th century, Yves Saint Laurent began with the purest and simplest examples of tubular furniture before tackling Dunand or Eileen Gray, Karl Lagerfeld had a more luxurious, perhaps more exotic, approach to Art Deco… It was our role as merchants to discover and buy the objects, get them out of the context of the flea market and bring them to the Left Bank, a strategy which has been copied since." The typically Parisian clientele was followed by an international panel of museums, especially German museums and American foundations such as the Sydney and Frances Lewis Foundation, which later donated its collection to the Atlanta Museum, or the de Ménil Foundation which bought cast iron pieces by Hector Guimard, and later the Japanese museums.

Félix Marcilhac likes Majorelle as much as Ruhlmann but confesses to a weakness for the creations of decorators such as Rateau, Groult and Jean-Michel Frank, or architects who designed furniture such as Printz and Chareau. He excludes from this epicurean eclecticism tubular chrome furniture à la Le Corbusier. "I think that in the field of Art Deco, you need to retain a certain sense of humor and fantasy, as was the case with Jacques Lejeune who worked at *Comoglio* and combined turn-of-the-century style with Napoleon III and beautiful neo-classical woodwork. Art Deco is being taken much too seriously today, there is too much pontificating. All the stores in the neighborhood have the same spot-lamps, the same screens, the same beige color."

Will Félix Marcilhac return to his first loves as a student, the plastic follies of the 1960s and 1970s? For the moment, he is content to redecorate his showroom on the Rue Bonaparte in bright colors, as a reminder that these were the Roaring Twenties and to show that through Majorelle, Art Nouveau is still capable of astonishing the passer-by.

PIERRE PASSEBON

Galerie du Passage, 1er arr.

"When I came to Paris in 1970, I pressed my nose against the window of Félix Marcilhac's store to gaze longingly at the *Chambre aux nénuphars* (room with waterlilies), by Majorelle. This was the epitome of elegance for me, just as I was fascinated by the window of Madeleine Castaing's store, a little further up the street, but I would never have dared enter the store."

Pierre Passebon began his working life as a publisher, opening his own publishing house, Éditions des Autres, whose authors included Pascal Bruckner. "I never thought of setting up as a merchant and then I agreed to look after the stand of a friend, Christian Sapet, at the Marché aux Puces. That was the beginning." He went to work for Christian Sapet, who was reigning over Paul Bert, and learned a great deal. "His eccentric taste shaped mine,

PASSEBON
Stone sculpture by Orlandini (Italy, 1920), cornice chair by Fornassetti (1950). The mosaic and the cornice are Roman. The bronze stag is a Napolitan cast from Antiquity. Contemporary chandelier by Ounouh, lamp by Alexandre Noll.

along with Marc Lamouric, who would combine Legrain furniture with African artefacts and Chinese silverware in the western taste." Next, Pierre Passebon went to the Left Bank, to work briefly with Joëlle-Mortier Vallat. The 19th-century furniture and *fin-de-siècle* paintings in the realistic style created an interior reminiscent of those by Louise Abbéma. Then he discovered the Passage Véro-Dodat, "the most beautiful passageway in Paris," where there were only modest stores and workshops, until a first antique dealer, Pierre Capia, led the way with his antique dolls, followed by Eric Philippe.

In Passebon's *Galerie du Passage:* large figurative paintings by Yakovlev, painter of the Black Crusade of the 1920s, serving as a background to a garden seat by the Art Nouveau ceramist Emile Muller, straw-seated metal chairs by Jean-Michel Frank, and a large porcelain by Josef Wackerle, the neo-rococo sculptor from Munich who flourished in the 1920s. Along with neo-Greek button-upholstered seating designed by Robsjohn-Gibbings for the Villa Incantada, egg-shaped chairs by Jean Royère, antique cast-iron deer from Naples that Coco Chanel liked… a mixture of the unusual and the strange, the decorative and the original, the classical and the modern, which deliberately escapes any strict classification. "I've never wanted to separate the ancient from the modern or specialize in a single esthetic category," explains Pierre Passebon, who has organized some memorable exhibitions. The exhibition devoted to Jean Royère in 1992, accompanied by a magnificent catalog which became a classic of its time, was one of the first rediscoveries of an artist who at the time had not yet been granted the acclaim he deserved. The display of the work of Christian Bérard, an artist whom Pierre Passebon discovered through Jean-Michel Frank, enabled one to see some important canvases such as the portrait of Marie-Laure de Noailles. The designer Emilio Terry was also the subject of an exhibition which displayed his so-called "astrologer's" furniture. Or the retrospective of Alexandre Noll's works in 1999, when the first monograph of the artist was published by the Éditions du Regard.

Despite his love for the contemporary, Pierre Passebon is not a minimalist. "I like warm modernism," he laughs, such as the wooden chairs by Charlotte Perriand or the anonymous English chairs of the Arts and Crafts Movement. To give free reign to his modernist taste, Passebon has also shown contemporary designers of furniture and objects such as Marcial Berro, an Argentinian artist, who uses his goldsmith's skill and refinement in the creation of furniture, the Americans Paul Mathieu and Michael Ray, Patrice Dangel, who works with bronze, or the cabinet-maker Vincent Corbière whose refined furniture he is fond of. The *Galerie du Passage* is the preferred place of many international decorators.

ÉRIC PHILIPPE

Galerie Éric Philippe, 1ᵉʳ arr.

"Pratically nothing predestined me for this profession. I was interested in art, fashion, and photography." A modest statement that says a lot about Éric Philippe. A critical eye, a feeling for the evolution of of taste–not much more was needed to turn to antique dealing. A friend of his in the fashion industry took a booth at the Marché aux Puces, and he hunted around in London and Marrakesh to build up her stock. This was in the early 1970s.

"At the time," Éric Philippe explains, "I was very interested in architects' furniture in metal, the Bauhaus." This was a taste shared by showbiz and fashion circles. "Then my tastes changed. I got tired of metal and became interested in wood and French Art Deco. I'm probably one of the first to take an interest in Jean-Michel Frank." This was the Frank of commonplace materials, who worked in wood, plaster and straw. Philippe left it to the

(Preceding pages)
PASSEBON
In the foreground, a pedestal table by Méret Oppenheim (edited circa 1960), sofa *Vague* by Jean Royère and Dolly (a Parson terrier). Rope tapestry by Calder. Head and veiled woman, designs by Bob Elia. Standard lamp *Jet d'eau* by Jean Royère. On the shelves of a bookcase by Jean-Michel Frank there is a set of sculptures by Alexandre Noll. Armchair by Ernest Boiceau (1930) and an eggshell coffee table by Jean Dunand (1930).

PHILIPPE
Carl Malmsten, a pair chairs in Cuba mahagony and holly-wood chairs. Stockholm, 1925.

well-heeled dealers to favor the fishskin and parchment. "I felt that three well-proportioned lines in sanded oak were enough." For him, the members of the Union of Modern Artists were too radical, systematic, and ideological—even those as brilliant as Pierre Chareau—and the decorators Jacques-Émile Ruhlmann and Jean Dunand, worked in materials that were too rich. He still prefers Jean-Michel Frank the artist and poet who knows how to orchestrate the colors of Christian Bérard, the shapes of the Giacometti brothers, and the allusions of Emilio Terry.

In the late 1970s, Philippe used a loft in Buttes-Chaumont area for an exhibition dedicated to Jean-Charles Moreux, Paul Dupré-Lafon and André Arbus for his refined classicism. "It was an era of sectarian tastes. If a table's legs weren't recilinear, that was considered a major disaster." When he opened his gallery in the Passage Véro-Dodat in 1979, his interest for the Wiener Werkstätte and Dagobert Peche set him on a road that was both more classical and more lyrical. He turned to Italy in the 20s with Gio Ponti (furniture in sycomore and granite) or Umberto Bellotto (imaginary objects in beaten iron). Next came Scandinavia, where designers had preserved a classic, even ancient tradition at the very core of their modernity as early as the 1910s. Through the magazine *Die Kunst,* he discovered Swedish Art Deco, the furniture designed by Carl Hörvik for the 1925 exhibition, that of Axel Einar Hjort for the Swedish pavillion in Barcelona in 1929 and the architecture of Erik Gunnar Asplund. "In Sweden, the styles arrive purified, filtered and create a light and dreamlike mix with local tradition." He also sought this allusive poetry in Danish and German Art Deco of the beginning of the 20s, and found it in France with the work of André Arbus, Ernest Boiceau, Henri Gonse, Bolette Natanson, and Serge Roche.

Éric Philippe knows how to convey to his clients his quest for purity and eclectism. There are very few objects in his gallery, and they are presented with an almost Japanese austerity. There are no period sets but items which are in the same spirit, regardless of origin. Éric holds one-man shows—Jean-Michel Frank in 1980, Ernest Boiceau in 1982, André Arbus in 1987, T.H. Robsjohn-Gibbings in 2000—or thematic exhibitions such as *Italian Artists 1900 to 1950* in 1986, *Swedish Grace* in 1998. These are accompanied by what he calls "collections," objects whose diversity reveals a collector's taste, his own.

(preceding pages)
PHILIPPE
Left: Axel Einar Hjortbirch sofa, canework and silk, Stockholm, 1928. *Right:* Macassar ebony, limewood and buxwood table by Carl Malmsten (Stockholm, 1925). Big carpet in *point noué* by Alf Munthe, woven by Elsa Gullberg (Stockholm, 1930)

ARNAUD PLAISANCE

Galerie Plaisance, 6ᵉ arr.

Plaisance was a law student who had also attended the ESIAG (private school of business administration), but a pal of his had a booth at the Marché aux Puces that he wanted to share, so his next step was inevitable. From the Serpette market at Saint-Ouen, adapting to the customs of the Parisian trade through a store in the Passage Véro-Dodat, then to a move to the Rue Bonaparte. It was the classic itinerary for a dealer in 1940s merchandise.

"It so happened that I fell in love with two Italian glass vases," recalls Arnaud Plaisance. "I tried to find out about them, and discovered Venini, Seguso, Barrovié-Toso… I became a specialist and since then, I always have had a hundred or so on permanent display. As for the rest, I learned on the job, meaning I made plenty of mistakes. At the Marché aux Puces, you buy on instinct, everything moves so fast. You have to wait to reach to the store to be able to start sorting things out and have time to think."

It is while he had a store in the Passage Véro-Dodat that Plaisance began to take an interest in the 1940s. "I remembered a clothestand by Dupré Lafond, it was affordable merchandise." He discovered the important names: René Drouet, Jean Pascaud, Dominique.

PLAISANCE
Opposite: Three oak X-framed armchairs by Félix Davin, the backs are adorned with *point de Cornélie* tapestry. Venetian iridescent glass chandelier *Caravelle* by Seguso Vetri d'Arte and produced by Veronese.

His arrival on the Rue Bonaparte meant geographical proximity to Yves Gastou, whose passions he shared, and enabled him to reach a wider private clientele and confirm his own taste. "I have a preference for more neo-classical things. I don't like baroque. I like neo-Louis XVI." The price inflation in 1940s items did not cause him to go for later objects, quite the opposite. "The quality of the craftmanship declined in the 1950s. I would be more inclined to go back to classic furniture of the Ruhlmann type."

Plaisance's "secret garden" is sculpture of the 20th century, the neoclassical school derived from the work of Charles Despiau and Hubert Yencesse. "It is major art but which is difficult to sell today, and I prefer for the moment to keep it for myself." Another little-known area he exhibits and defends is that of modern tapestry of the 1930s to 1950s, the "Aubusson revival" with names such as Jean Lurçat, Jean Picart Le Doux… "Easy trading bores me. Since I had a booth at the flea market, I know what sells and what doesn't. If you want to sell standardized goods, you might as well start selling cars."

JOSEPHA AND MÉLODIE POKORNY

M. Danbon-J. Pokorny, 7ᵉ arr.

By antique-hunting, one turns into an antique-hunter. Josepha Pokorny started at the Village Suisse, "where we sold English pine furniture" but didn't like what she saw there, preferring to hunt for antiques after hours with friends who were also dealers, such as Chantal Rodary and Pierre Moinot. Alongside the pine, she built up a little stock of good "18th to 19th century." But things really started to move when she accepted a bet. "It was when there were those Saint-Germain-des-Prés parties. One evening, I made a bet with Anne-Sophie Duval, who at the time already had a store on the Quai Malaquais. If I lost, I would have to look after her store for a week. I lost the bet, but I gained a fantastic experience, because I stayed with her for ten years." That is how Josepha discovered the 20h century through someone who was born into the trade, the daughter of Yvette Barran, one of the ground-breakers for Art Nouveau. "Anne-Sophie Duval had the eye of a pioneer who can spot the great creators before she even knows their names." It was perfect training. "It was through her that I developed my taste for 20th-century ceramics," which was to become one of her specialities.

She has been on her own for the past ten years. She was one of the first to give the Rue de Lille its "20th cen-tury" look, initially with the decorator Françoise Lafon then, more recently, with her daughter Mélodie Danbon whom she taught the trade. She expanded her taste for Art Nouveau to a European scope including British, Viennese and also Italian artists, such as Paolo Buffa and Gio Ponti. She is interested in the shape, the lines of furniture, which enables her to place a neo-classical Thonet next to a 19th-century Chinese console table or an easel by Sornay that is "as beautiful as a Cubist sculpture." This does not prevent her from falling for the fragile charms of a pastel-colored Venetian mirror. Her ceramics and stoneware, whether isolated or grouped, indicate the extent of her interest which focus mainly on France and Denmark. The Nordic esthetics, a mixture of classicism and folk tradition, fascinates her. She discovered a Swedish carpet designer, Marta Maas Fjetterstrom, and went to see her work *in situ* in order to be able to understand it better. "What is great about this occupation is that you learn something new every day, even by making mistakes. You remain curious, eager to know. You're always discovering something new. I don't know how to talk about my occupation, but I just love to listen."

POKORNY
Plaster mirror by Sébastien (1938). Ormolu enameled vase (1930), sold at the Rouard shop. Two ceramic vases by Jacques Ruelland (1960).

MAROUN H. SALLOUM

Maroun H. Salloum, 7ᵉ arr.

Saloum spent his childhood in Lebanon, then studied fine arts and decorative art in France, and thought he might like to design furniture. He was a student in architecture when he got started in the antique business: he was rummaging in an antique shop and came across a Roman foot in marble "which still had a few bits of bronze sticking to the calves." He managed to scrape the money together to pay for it and then thought: Why not become a dealer myself? Antiques won out over his studies, marking the start of the adventure.

"I would buy Greco-Roman pieces in London and resell them in Paris, but people were always asking me how old I was." Unfortunately, the market was already too well structured and the clientele consisted of a few specialists, so Maroun Saloum turned his attention to the Renaissance. He travelled throughout Italy, acquiring bronzes, glassware, textiles, and fabrics: "It may have been Fortuny, whose fabrics I discovered, who triggered my liking for what I call influenced furniture, revisited styles, exoticism." He also loves a variety of materials–such as Arte Povera, straw inlays, painted furniture, gilded rocaille–and a variety of styles: Turkish style, chinoiserie, Russian romanticism, "Madeleine Castaing's château style," between Ferrières and Groussay, a taste similar to that of the decorator Jean-Paul Faye.

Saloum finds himself incapable of specializing or choosing between various tastes: "I prefer to be surrounded with what I like, and then sort through it. I never sell anything immediately." Hence the usefulness of his storage facility which was once the studio of the painter Ingres, below his home, a stone's throw from his gallery on the Rue de Lille. This is where everything is laid out and arranged, where the surprises and revelations happen. He is inconstant and fickle, choosing items as the fancy takes him, when he happens to spot something interesting on one of his trips or through a chance encounter. Despite his Mediterranean origins, Saloum has a penchant for Mittel Europa and its Art Nouveau–the Secessionists, Wiener Werkstätte, Berlage and the Amsterdam school. "I was astonished by the architecture in Budapest and I looked for objects that matched the architecture of Odon Lechner, such as the large ornamental basins produced by the factory in Zsolnay, in a sort of barbarian, opulent, neo-Attila style." He is a fervent admirer of Josip Plecnic, with whose work in Ljubljana he is particularly familiar and of Lajos Kozma, the Hungarian Ruhlmann. The Drouot auction rooms and rummaging in the French provinces seem more remote to him than Prague, Munich, or Buenos Aires and he prefers the abandoned, wrecked furniture of some distant castle in the Carpathians to all the mahogany furniture of the French ports.

Naturally, Maroun Saloum's clients are his sort of people, cosmopolitan travellers who claim no country as their own. They create a new world for themselves in shapes and colors which only a foreign eye could appreciate, such as the Bruno Paul furniture which is out of favor in the country that invented Bauhaus but which on the Rue de Lille, regains the spice of the strangely out-of-place. No country, no material, no period of 20th-century Europe escapes the comparisons of this hectic antique dealer who draws similarities between Venetian wrought iron by Belloto and that of the Parisian Eugène Grasset, and who prefers the *Buxus* furniture of Gino Levi Montallini and Guiseppe Pagano Pogatschnig to the plastic things of the 1970s. With the help of designers such as Richard Peduzzi, Maroun Saloum is amongst those who have shaken up the traditional Biennale, forcing it to turn outward to Europe and to embrace the 20th century.

SALLOUM
Opposite: In the foreground, wrought-iron throne by Umberto Bellotto (Venice, 1914) and a mantelpiece by Bellery-Desfontaine, 1907. Chandelier by Gio Ponti, 1940. On the table by Paul Dupré Lafon (circa 1940), two nickel-plated brass heads by Franz Hagenauer (Vienna, 1920) and a bronze by Arno Breker, 1911. On the two-piece furniture by Bellery-Desfontaine, sits a 17th-century lacquer Buddha from Birmany.

(following pages)
SALLOUM
Left: In the foreground, a chair in oak and Brazilian rosewood (Vienna, 1920). Behind, a waxed oak armchair by Richard Riemerschmid, circa 1908. Against the back wall, two Czech Cubist armchairs of 1925 on either side of a chest by Umberto Bellotto (circa 1915) on which stands a glazed stoneware basin by Strobl Alajos (manufactory of Zsolnay, Hungary, 1904). A pair of solid oak cases, inspired by African art, by Herbert Ward, circa 1905.
Right: Portrait of *Rembrandt Bugatti* by Carlo Bugatti, 1908. Glazed stoneware jar by Paul Wynand (Germany, 1910).

PATRICK SERRAIRE

Patrick Serraire, 7ᵉ arr.

"Since you paint all day, why don't you come and look after the gallery every morning between ten and twelve?" "Two weeks later, I had stopped painting, and I had opened a 19th-century department in the gallery of my friend Philippe Ratton who specialized in African art." Patrick Serraire is someone who makes abrupt changes in his life. Once he has found a new direction, he totally embraces it and takes it to the ultimate. "You must be professional in everything you do."

He is a graduate of the Charpentier Academy, the Camondo School at Philippe Starck's studio. He has an almost maniacal penchant for precision: "I did the best drawings." His gods are Klinger and Böcklin, his inspiration comes from Jean Lorrain, Huysmans, and Wilde, the estheres and magicians revealed by Philippe Jullian. From the Symbolists to the Surrealists and the Realists of the 1930s, with no concession being made for this own times. But you have to make a living, so Patrick Serraire became a photographer in advertising. Then, for five years, he did nothing but paint "with a thread-counter and magnifying glass," producing a large painting every three months, working twelve hours a day, with an acute, obsessional insight. In 1979, Philippe Ratton's offer launched him on the path of the Symbolists and Pre-Raphaelites. He admired a different type of sculptor, though—Frémiet, Gerôme, Saint Marceaux, and Stuck—, and the nebulous turn-of-the-century European style of decorative art as practiced in Vienna, Glasgow, Darmstadt and Brussels.

Patrick Serraire loved structural detail, and the complex mechanisms of the lighting by Otto Wagner and William A. S. Benson. He was also interested in the combination of materials, such as the ways Wagner and Gustave Serrurier Bovy assembled wood and metal, and Bugatti's use of parchment and copper. Deep down inside, he was a restorer, who dismantled his treasured objects, then painstakingly reassembled them piece by piece with loving care. His pantheon included Josef Hoffmann (the Sitzmachine chair), Charles Rennie Mackintosh, as well as Georges Walton, Godwin, and Christopher Dresser. His love of ingenious simplicity did not prevent him from appreciating Grohé, Sormani, Viardot, and Lièvre, these master craftsmen of the industrial arts who loved to cross different styles and techniques in an ornamental flurry of marquetry and ormolu, pietra dura, enamels and electroplating. In his secret garden, he cultivated a few delicate artists such as Paul Iribe and Maurice Dufresne.

The success of the Ratton-Serraire duo brought them from the Rue de Grenelle to the Quai Voltaire, where the old clientele mingled with the new. Paradoxically, Patrick Serraire left the business once again. For three years, he became a mechanic and applied his patience to a new passion: old motorbikes which he assembled piece by piece in his apartment, amongst his personal collection of antiques, as if they were idols of steel, chrome and paintwork.

Serraire took up antique dealing again in 1993 and opened a store, on his own this time, on the Rue de Lille. Old passions were refound, and he refined his taste in the various English, Viennese, and German trends and their French counterparts, attracting several collectors and decorators who were as demanding as he was. In this neighborhood which has been welcoming dealers specializing in the period from the 1940s to the 1970s, Patrick Serraire stands out as a veteran "at the sources of the 20th century."

SERRAIRE
In the foreground, a chair by Serrurier Bovy (prototype, 1904). Two German (?) wardrobes (circa 1905-1910). Two chairs by Joseph Hoffmann (circa 1910), the two frames are German (circa 1905-1910). On the pedestal table by Joseph Hoffmann (1904), there is a lamp by Ilrin (France, circa 1905).

BOB AND CHESKA VALLOIS

Vallois, 6ᵉ arr.

"One day, Bob arrived with two Breuer chairs. I looked at them and inquired: 'What are these?' He replied: 'I don't know, I came across them and was told they were made in the 1920s.' I said to him: 'I love this stuff.' Today, I wouldn't give them a second glance, but they made me want to find out what was going on at the time. Bob must have been very surprised to find me excited by a couple of tubes."

Bob Vallois was the antique-hunter and Cheska ran the little store in Cap-d'Ail on the French Riviera. The stock consisted of Louis-Philippe, Napoleon III, turn-of-the-century glassware, and "trinkets"–right up until 1970, when Les Halles, the Parisian wholesale market, moved. It was just the time to find 400 sq. metres in Paris, on the Rue Saint-Denis. "We worked like crazy to pay the rent and tried to learn as much as we could. We did research at the Forney Library and visited the Decorative Arts Museum to educate our eye, then went off to the Marché aux Puces." They concentrated on a few well-known names, such as Ruhlmann and Dunand. A year later, a stupendous find catapulted them into the center of a new market. They discovered fifteen items of furniture made by Eileen Gray for Madame Talbot, including the famous gondola and the large low piece now in the collection of Yves Saint Laurent. "We were hoping, without really believing it, that it was a Dunand piece, but we couldn't find a mark or a signature. There was no price-list for Art Deco at the time. When Bob Walker, an English collector, told us it was a piece by Eileen Gray, we were horribly disappointed. He explained it to us, we read up on it, I even met with Eileen Gray. Our path had been traced. We were lucky enough to find real materpieces which indelibly create one's taste."

The Vallois left the store they had set up in 1971 at 15, Rue Saint-Denis ten years later, crossing over to the Left Bank. The Jacques Doucet sale of 1972 ignited a market that was still practically inexistent, the names of Marcel Coard, Pierre Legrain, and Eileen Gray becoming known outside the small circle of dealers to initiate a tiny band of clients. In the late 1970s, the Vallois discovered Jean-Michel Frank, a passion which they shared with Jacques Grange, Yves Saint Laurent and Pierre Bergé. Their place of worship was the large reception rooms of the Hôtel des Noailles, on the Place des États-Unis, with their mixture of austerity and opulence. "The Americans also became enthusiastic, first the dealers, then the collectors. Frank was and remains the authority." This did not prevent the Vallois from becoming excited about other designers which were then less well-known, such as Armand-Albert Rateau. "We must have bought our first piece of Rateau furniture at Enghien in 1982, a bronze dressing table, and I subsequently developed a real passion for his work. As soon as you buy a piece and start to live with it, you start to see it differently, to break it down into its elements. I waited until 1986 to exhibit at my first Biennale, where I showed four pieces of furniture by Rateau, and I have never stopped buying his work."

The Art Deco market has expanded in the past thirty years. On both sides of the Atlantic, the new generations have learned to recognize quality, but Iribe, Rateau, Gray, and Legrain are reserved for an elite clientele. "Today, the real problem for dealers in Art Deco is not to find clients, but to find objects." Are the Vallois tempted to deal in later 20th-century items? They claim that it is hard to find the same quality in subsequent years, in materials, design, and inventiveness, but they would not hesitate to buy "an exceptional object, such as the recent purchase of four wall lamps by Poillerat which are sublime and timeless." They have just bought a gallery in New York.

VALLOIS
On the plaster fireplace by Alberto Giacometti for Jean-Michel Frank, there is a plaster lamp by Jean-Michel Frank and a pair of elephants by Paul Iribe. A wall lamp in the shape of a fan by Jacques-Émile Ruhlmann.

VALLOIS

Above: The chair is by Pierre Chareau. On the metal smoking table by Pierre Chareau,
a vase by Jean Dunand. *Opposite:* In front of the lacquer screen by Eileen Gray, two vases
by Jean Dunand on a table decorated with mother-of-pearl inlay by Jean-Michel Frank.
The carpet is by Da Silva Bruhns. On the wall, a pair of plaster wall lamps by Diego Giacometti.

OLIVIER WATELET

Galerie Olivier Watelet, 6ᵉ arr.

A shared love of the French Empire and the Directoire, for mahogany and sabre armchairs has given Olivier Watelet and Matthieu de Prémont their personal vision of the 20th century. "When I was a child, my grandmother would take me to visit the antique dealers in the Village Suisse, such as Antoinette Héron de Villefosse. In my first store, I sold classical and neo-classical antiques," Olivier Watelet recalls. He began his career as a broker at Drouot for an ephemeral "consumers' association." Having heard that the Serpette flea market at St.-Ouen was expanding, he opened a booth there at the end of the 70s.

After studying acting, Matthieu de Prémont took advantage of the periods when he was "resting" to hunt for antiques at Drouot, especially the French Empire period. That was how he discovered Olivier Watelet, from whom he bought some collapsible travelling chairs. In the meantime, Watelet had moved into 20th-century items, which were more affordable for a beginner. But which part of the 20th century? He was neither attracted to the metal and tubes of the UAM nor to the precious materials and ornaments of Art Deco, finding the former too severe and the latter too bourgeois; in any case, these categories had already reached their peak. Making a virtue out of necessity, Olivier Watelet discovered Jacques Adnet's work of the late 1930s when he departed from modernism, someone named André Arbus, then a few things which at the time were considered "amusing," such as Gilbert Poillerat ironwork, lamps by Jean Royère and, even then, some of the work of Serge Roche.

On the one hand, he pursued a neo-classical look which was a thread running through the 20th century, and on the other, a more fantasmagorical vision. "I was taught by the Jesuits," explains Olivier Watelet, "and I retained a taste for strictness, but I needed to develop an antidote, to escape into a dream world of the imagination. I love the circus and Surrealism. I love Dominguez, Dalí, Delvaux, and Magritte." "I prefer Nicolas de Staël and Raoul Ubac," says Matthieu de Prémont who joined Olivier Watelet in 1985. "For a while, I considered continuing my acting career, then I spent my free time at the Forney Library, to gain a deeper knowledge of the 1930s and 1940s. That is how we discovered Jacques Quinet, who is a bit our house artist."

Two public sales of Quinet works in 1982 and 1984 and a few scattered magazine articles enable them to understand the discreet personality of a creator who began with an allusive classicism in the 1940s, but who, after a long period of refining his style, went on to a more poetic design in wood, metal, and leather. "The quality of his work has been exceptional throughout his career and remains of high quality even in the furniture produced in small series." They were curious enough about him to want to meet his family and, by looking them up in the telephone book, they arranged a meeting with someone who claimed to have known him well. They thus discovered an elderly, mischievous man who eventually admitted to them: "I am Jacques Quinet." Their gallery opening in 1988 was dedicated to him. "People looked at us in amazement. It was too purified, too late." Now that his work has been exhibited at the Biennale and the gallery has commissioned a monograph, Jacques Quinet has entered the pantheon of great designers of the 20th century. This has not prevented the two antique dealers from retaining a fondness for Serge Roche, his fairy-tale world of enchanted castles, and for Emilio Terry whose taste for a purified neo-classicism was theirs from the start.

OLIVIER WATELET
A pair of plaster floor lamps by Serge Roche (circa 1934) and a *tête-à-tête* seat by Jansen (circa 1945).

CHAPTER 4

HIGH
CURIOSITY

AKKO VAN ACKER

Akko van Acker, 7ᵉ arr.

Once upon a time, in the 1960s, there was a handsome young man who was eager to leave his family and the cloudy skies of his native Holland. His destination was the Côte d'Azur, for sea, sun, and sand: Cannes and Saint-Tropez, four months of doing nothing, just beachcombing, a very long *après-midi d'un faune.* But his savings melted away in the sun, so when an antique dealer in the Rue Bonaparte in Paris offered him an internship, Akko Van Acker agreed to return to civilization, learn French and study Art History at the École du Louvre. In the evenings, he socialized with fellow dealers in the neighborhood–Grognot and Joinel, Raymond Poteau, Madeleine Castaing.

His first deal, which involved a painting bought in the flea market, revealed Van Acker's innate talents as a businessman, but he could not bear to give up the climate of the South of France, so in 1967, he settled in a little fisherman's cottage in Saint-Tropez. At first, he made a living selling painted furniture–stylish rustic–searching for items throughout his native Holland or in the local area in his subcompact car. Then his numerous London friends, Geoffroy Benisson in particular, and Guy Thodoroff, a great collector, initiate him to atypical furniture, large portraits, blue-and-white wares, lacquered furniture, and Blue Johns, antiques very much "in the style of the Royal Pavillion at Brighton." Van Acker only worked for three months out of the year, but eventually his business streak won out over the beach.

He opened his first store on the Rue de l'Université on the edge of the "Carré des Antiquaires" bounded by the Left Bank and the Boulevard Saint-Germain. Since then, he has moved no further than the other side of the street. He has exhibited at a few Biennales, created some startling window displays, and presented some provocative exhibitions, while conserving his youth and his tan. He is something of a cult figure–envied and even imitated. The copycats who surround him soon acquired the nickname of "Akkotés."

Van Acker's first Biennale in 1988 revealed the secret of his success to the wider public: a mixture of simplicity and excess. There was pinewood flooring, bleached woodwork, and plain or painted wooden furniture–all disproportionately large: seating for giants, chests of drawers that were too long, and bookshelves that stretched on endlessly. In a sophisticated clutter, an accumulation of objects and books, a collection of ivory parrots, lacquer

VAN ACKER

Above: Painted sheet metal tulips of the 19th century. *Sang-de-bœuf* (bloodred) vase, 19th century. Collection of *papier-mâché* flowers, scientific models, 19th century. *Opposite:* Neoclassical vase in Egyptian alabaster, early 19th century. *Following pages: Portrait de gentilhomme* by Kroll (Austria, 18th century). Bunch of flowers in *petit point* (England, circa 1880). The cast-iron stag is by the American sculptor G. Fiscke. Huge American mahagony "masterchair," 18th century.

ware and large, improbable portraits, plus a taste for weird materials–lacquered porcelain, imitation ceramics in wood, painted sheet metal. There are pieces of architecture or decor and paintings of fantastic or subtly erotic subjects. He has the taste of the curious, of a hedonist and a jet-setter who likes to hunt for antiques in Los Angeles, Miami, Brussels, Amsterdam, London, Munich, Milan or even at the Porte de Pantin flea market.

This restless traveller likes objects that are out of context, displaced, exiled or exported, designed by Daniel Marot in Holland or by the Chinese for export. He can only tolerate French antiques if there is something un-usual about them. "I would never buy a dining room table to seat twelve, I would never buy a French Regency curved chest of drawers or a flat Louis XV desk because there are already two or three hundred such items for sale in Paris. When I attended the Biennales, I looked for the most outstanding paintings, a magnificent 17th-century dog, or Japanese ivory parrots, objects that you never see." These items from all over the place are art-fully arranged in the store on the Rue de l'Université by Riccardo Wilhelmsen, with whom Van Acker has been working for nearly twenty years. His perfect skills of presentation and positioning have made "Van Akker's attic" a pleasure for the eye and a paradise for Laziz Hamani.

NICOLE ALTÉRO

Galerie Altéro, 7ᵉ arr.

Nicole Altéro was born on the Quai Voltaire, right over her mother's shop, so she knows the story of her neigh-borhood: "When my Mom arrived, there were nothing but dealers in prints and books. My grandmother was horrified at the idea of our living on the Left Bank, which she believed to be full of charlatans. The honest deal-ers were all in the 8th arrondissement." Only a few galleries kept the tradition of the quayside alive. There was Buvelot with his decorations, Gabrielle Lorie and Antonia de la Gandara who were the first, along with Madeleine Castaing, to offer "amusing" 19th-century pieces. Madame Bella Gamba, who sold tapestries, and Thenadey, who had had a store at the corner of the Rue des Saints-Pères since the 1930s. A few doors down, an antique dealer had recreated a Spanish cloister in his courtyard. Further on, the "shacks" of the Rue des Saints-Pères,–on the site of what is now the Faculty of Medicine–housed such dealers as Lefebvre and Nicolier, the future greats of the Left Bank.

Nicole's mother concentrated on the 18th century, displaying fabrics, tableware, fans, porcelain from *La Compagnie des Indes* (The French India Company), and small Louis XV and Louis XVI pieces of furniture. Carmen Altéro called her store *Galerie Pompadour* and specialized in old glass. Nicole did not go through the usual teenage revolt: "I loved the trade, and played at it when I was really young. First I worked unpacking things at the flea market, then came to give Mom a hand. I then took over the store in 1980."

Nicole continued to concentrate on antique glassware. The specialist museums, such as the Corning Museum, know her well. She has a preference for Murano or "Murano-style" glass, German engraved glass and old flasks or bottles. She also continues the tradition of tableware but is guided by her own love of European lacquer-ware, mirrors and China export painting under glass, as well as 17th-century plated metal vases or ewers. She has a weakness for fragile, subtle materials, such as objects or furniture inlaid with straw maquetry and spotted Italian tortoiseshell but she has given a more virile note to the gallery by bringing in Louis XIV pieces, marble basins, and monumental andirons with decorated figures. She also has some terra cotta sculptures and small bronzes. There is not much marquetry or gilded wood, but painted and sometimes lacquered French, Provence or Italian furniture.

NICOLE ALTÉRO
Mirror from Sardinia. Neoclassical console (Italy, circa 1750). Brocatello tabletop (Spain).

ALTÉRO

Above: Glassware from the 18th century: an engraved ewer with a pewter top, a sprinkler with a screw-on cap,
a cut and engraved flask (France). *Opposite:* An opaline carafe with medallion (Portugal, 18th century), an opaline bottle
(Germany, 18th century), a cup *Orléans* by Bernard Perrot, with enameled birds (late 17th century).

The graceful arrangement of the gallery often inspires her customers, who are usually friends, to ask for Nicole's advice on matters of interior design. In Paris, like in Provence, her style has a lightness and is composed of harmonies of white, beige, and gray against which a few muted colors play. "I am not a decorator *per se*. I find fabrics and comfortable furniture and I arrange them in the right place." She often uses the Carré Rive Gauche exhibition to display her favorite objects–mirrors, for example. On these occasions, Nicole transforms her gallery, with the aid of mosses and flowers which she knows better than anyone, into enchanted pavilions, which tends to disrupt the traffic along the quayside.

JEAN-FRANÇOIS DE BLANCHETTI

Jean-François de Blanchetti, 7ᵉ arr.

Jean-François de Blanchetti is from Nice and originally studied agronomy, spending time with the gauchos on the cattle ranches of Argentina before entering the art market. He obtained his auctoneer's diploma with flying colors, but decided not to enter the profession and instead worked with Juan Portela, who was one of the first dealers to bring "charm and comfort" to the Quai Voltaire in the 1980s. Blanchetti opened his own store a stone's throw away at the beginning of the Rue des Saints-Pères. When you enter his store, it feels like you're visiting a private home. Here is furniture that looks as though it has just been removed from a stately home and not from a restorer's workshop. The mahogany has acquired the patina of age, the armchairs have retained their *petit point* embroidery, the large, leather, buttoned sofas are ready to be installed at your fireside, and the Venetian chandelier has not yet been converted to electricity. The stock is not flashy or showy; it is solid and comfortable. Here, one can dream of being at home among family souvenirs and memories of far-off places from every era and every style, with that aura of mystery and charm worn by objects bought for their appeal.

DE BLANCHETTI
On the mahogany table (Belgium, circa 1900) a watercolor showing the *Procession of the pontifical coach* (circa 1830). The English mahogany sofa, in Queen Ann style, is from the 19th century. A series of four colored engravings after Monpezat, *La vie d'un gentilhomme en toutes saisons.* Mirror made of pale wood and pair of gilt iron consoles from the 1940s.

Jean-François de Blanchetti knows this type of home well and he likes to furnish it slowly, with his customers' help, according to his wanderings and discoveries. He has never indulged in the "shabby chic" favored by readers of *Interior's,* although he knows what well-tanned leather is and the color of Trianon gray. He may be nostalgic for the Forties, and his references would be Bagues, Jansen, or the firm of Toulouse, those fine suppliers who were able to take the great inventions of the past and adapt them to the fashion of the day: furniture in antiqued mirror and palm-tree rocaille chests of drawers which Daisy Fellowes the Duchess of Windsor would have liked for their country houses. Other examples would be Groussay's library and bedrooms. Blanchetti loves to create for others the home he would have liked to have for himself in those days when he dreamed of becoming a gentleman farmer.

LUC BOUVERET

Luc Bouveret, 7ᵉ arr.

"First antechamber, second antechamber, gallery." The existing space had to be unified in order to create a succession of rooms, like in a palace. "I wanted the decor to reflect a taste for the 18th century, but in a modern light," admits Luc Bouveret. The gallery is not paneled, but there are large panels of red damask framed in gilt moulding against a fake stone background. The doors are covered in blue silk. The marble floor of the entrance, large garlands in Delafosse or Ledoux style lay down the rules of strict classicism. A full-length portrait of the

BOUVERET

Above: At the foot of the full-length *Portrait of the Count of Toulouse,* a pair of Chinese porcelain pedestal tables lacquered
"Chinese style" (France, circa 1670). *Opposite:* In the foreground, two wooden gilt chairs by Georges Jacob (master in 1765).
On the Louis XIV armchair made of gilt walnut and covered with a patterned tapestry, sits Olympe (a Jack Russel terrier).
To the left, a Regency timepiece in ebony.

Count of Toulouse as a child, pointing at his fleet on the horizon. Above the gilt wooden console table there is a decorative wall-clock. Facing are three marble profiles of the Empire period, and a marble bacchante on a Louis XVI console table. Amid this princely decor, created by Jacques Garcia, there are a few items of furniture of notable origin, such as the tall chest with seven drawers "which is branded with the mark of Marie-Antoinette at the Trianon," and others which prefer to remain incognito, such as this secretary by Riesener, "very architectural, unbelievably modern, perhaps not opulent enough to be sought after." In the course of a few years, Luc Bouveret has made an unfaltering progression, from the flea market to the Place de Furstemberg, then to the Rue de l'Université, and finally to the Quai Voltaire, where he is the youngest dealer.

Bouveret's career began when he decided to abandon the office life where his diploma in business studies from the *École Supérieure de Commerce* had landed him. He served an apprenticeship with a friend who restored and sold rustic furniture, then set up a booth in the Marché aux Puces where he sold painted furniture around which he created settings admired by his clients. "I used to sell whole rooms." Then he moved to the Left Bank and hunted in Italy for Venetian furniture, gilt wood and marble profiles. His feeling for decoration and pretty things evoked the pleasures of bygone times: such as an 18th-century pearl coin-purse, a lacquered box for a perfume flask, a wig-box, and a jewelry box in the shape of a miniature castle made of straw marquetry, whose roof and wall opened into several little compartments. There were "collectors' items," like his wax profiles. In short, merchandise that was "original, amusing, and decorative." Then came a desire to have "really fine pieces, beautiful furniture of the kind sought by connoisseurs and collectors."

The Quai Voltaire seemed to him to be the right place for this new venture, an elegant environment where he could receive connoisseurs looking for rare furniture, especially French. But "fine" does not mean "richly decorated." Luc Bouveret prefers well-proportioned pieces to those made of expensive materials, pure lines rather than "that furniture encrusted with marquetry and bronze." This does not prevent him from furnishing his own home with some contemporary pieces made by inventive designers who incorporate tradition into their creations and "leave their ego aside." Among his modern favorites are Hubert Le Gall and André Dubreuil, as well as Gladys Mougins and her disciples. He often drops into her gallery in the nearby Rue de Lille.

ALAIN DEMACHY

Galerie Camoin Antiquités, 7ᵉ arr.

The entrance is in Hollywood style, with dizzyingly high ceilings, bull's-eye windows, a spiral staircase whose walls are adorned with carpets and tapestries, then a series of reception rooms on the upper floor. A taste for opulence and a sense of proportion which hint that behind the antique dealer, there is a decorator and architect. It is through designing house interiors for clients that Alain Demachy came into the antiques trade. His grandfather was a picturalist photographer, his father, a painter and fashion artist. Their home was designed by Jean-Charles Moreux, and although the family setting was rather traditional, his taste ran to such modern artists as the Bauhaus group, Paul Klee, Vassily Kandinsky, and Fernand Léger.

Didier Aaron suggested that Alain Demachy work for his clients, then they joined forces in order to create a classic decoration business in same vein as Jansen or Barroux. He was surrounded by a new generation–Jacques Grange, Patrice and Anne Nourissat–whose style was still evolving. "I began to discover antiques through the merchants to whom I brought my clients. Nicolas Landau, Bensimon, Hamel–and, of course, Didier Aaron obviously taught me a lot." He also learned from some of his clients, such as Edmond de Rothschild: "I

182

CAMOIN-DEMACHY

Above: Ormolu helmet decorating one of the bedposts of a mahogany bed, commissioned by General Lecourbe from the maison Jacob Frères, circa 1804-1810. *Jeune fille créole,* carrying a basket on her head (terra cotta, 18th century). Gilt wooden armchairs, early 19th century.

Opposite: The winter garden. Garden furniture, Portuguese sofa made of painted wood, pedestal table with mother-of-pearl decor, French Napoleon III chandelier in *pâte-de-verre* and ormolu.

presented collections of ancient art for him or whole rooms of typical Boldini style, with black and gold, Second Empire furniture which had come from the Pereire family."

In the 70s, Alain Demachy took over the store which had belonged to Bernard Raynaud, an antique dealer of the old school on the corner of the Rue de Grenelle and the Rue de la Chaise. "It was fun having my own little boutique while continuing to work with Didier Aaron. I began to do some art dealing." He was one of the first to introduce to Paris the delightful neo-classicism he had found in Italy, Sweden, and England: mahogany furniture, ormolu, souvenirs of the "Grand Tour" and a bit of sculpture. "Rather the taste of a decorator, I won't deny it."

One day, while visiting Madame Camoin at her store on the Quai Voltaire, he told her: "If you ever want to leave here one day, I'd be interested." "It was totally unrealistic on my part, but in the end, the deal got done. I had acquired luxurious tastes through my clients, but I never had the means to purchase chests of drawers by Riesener or Joseph. I preferred to buy, in the same quality, large carpets, such as those made by the Savonnerie, or chandeliers which were not particularly sought after in the 1980s. That is how I was able to sell a carpet which had belonged to Louis XIV to a famous American woman."

An architect by training, Alain Demachy is more concerned with the proportions of furniture than the richness of its decoration. He shows a preference for unusual chairs: "It's probably he most inventive area because it's the most restricting as regards construction. A chair can always be surprising and have a personality, but a chest of drawers is just a chest of drawers."

The 20th century has contributed its touch of fantasy and exactness, a European mix of Jugendstil as well as Art Deco, Liberty and Wienerwerkstätte. The decorator and the antique dealer work on parallel paths without interfering with each other. "I did not give my name to the showroom in order to establish the distance." And thus *Camoin* is a must-see for foreign decorators, who like to bring their clients to this temple of quintessential Parisian taste.

ALAIN FINARD AND GÉRARD WAHL-BOYER
Galerie Alain & Gérard, 7ᵉ arr.

ALAIN ET GÉRARD
Opposite: In front of a Flemish 16th century stained-glass window showing *Adoration of the Magi,* a couple of dignitaries in terra cotta (China, Han dynasty).
Following pages: Left: In the foreground, an glazed earthenware apothecary jar (Montpellier, 16th century). On its left, a mug decorated with ivory sculptures with bronze top and base (Germany). In the background, on a console with a marble table-top, a pair of bronze mandarins from the Ming period. In front of the console, a celadon funerary urn, Song period.
Right: : detail of the head of a wooden Konso statue (Ethiopia, early 20th century).

They met at the ages of 17 and 18 and pursued similar careers in antique dealing. They had booths at the markets in Montreuil and Aligre (one whole square meter displaying a single object, a bronze by Barye). They then graduated to the Marché aux Puces: Alain Finard was at Paul Bert, Gérard Wahl-Boyer at Vernaison before they finally shared a booth in the late 60s. "At the time, the Puces were of various styles, but the merchandise consisted mainly of 18th-century plain wooden furniture or 19th-century pieces made for export. We were more interested in collectors' artefacts of any period. For the price of a Napoleon III mantelpiece ornament, we preferred to buy old bronzes or foreign ceramics. We bought miscellaneous wares, such as terra cotta, earthenware, lacquer, ivory items, and silverware."

They combed the country, picking through the stock of their fellow dealers in the provinces, just like plenty of other Parisian dealers. "When we left the flea market for the Left Bank, it was to reach connoisseurs in Paris and an international clientele." The mid-70s was the heyday of the neighborhood. "We had a mixed clientele: a lot of amateurs, small-scale collectors, as well as professionals. Unfortunately, today, some of the collectors and amateurs have disappeared."

Although Gérard is officially an expert in African art, his interests are not confined exclusively to that field—he

also knows a lot about Asian art, for example. Alain loves old bronzes, furniture of unusual proportions, such as the set of shelves by Canabas "a piece of furniture with nice, clean lines–perfect."

In their gallery, Alain and Gérard have their own approach to presentation and decoration. They remain faithful to the spirit of 19th-century *bric-à-brac,* preferring to let their wares blend in together and create their own harmony. Sometimes they almost get lost in the cluster, and it takez the sharp eye and the good ear of a real connoisseur (as Balzac's *Cousin Pons* would have said) to single them out. A medieval virgin, three Ming dynasty Buddhas, a Roman head, a Chinese finial, a model of a Louis XIV table centerpiece, a Renaissance marble profile, a German baroque copper wall lamp… Here it is the object that is important, rather than the decor and style. "You can't find stores like this any more," exclaimed an important dealer of the Right Bank who was visiting Alain et Gérard for the first time. It's a whimsical place, a timeless treasure trove which is keeping up the tradition of the curio dealer on the Left Bank.

PATRICK AND JOSÉPHINE FRÉMONTIER

Frémontier, 7ᵉ arr.

Along the noble and respectable Quai Voltaire, one of the bastions of the "curiosity" trade for the past two centuries, Patrick and Joséphine Frémontier have created in their store window since January 1990 some astonishing and jolting displays. There are monumental statues, cabinets weighed down in gilt and sculptures, rooms of mirrors or porcelain, disconcerting styles, exotic origins. A certain amount of daring was needed to break with the tradition of good form and good taste, and give these "curiosities," as these antiques were once known, their modern credentials. "The French are still obsessed with Louis XIV, as if Louis XIV was the final word. Thank goodness, being part of the European Community will help us escape the French taste." The Frémontiers have even coined the term "Franco-French" to designate timid French customers who need to be reassured with "authentic 18th-century."

"'When I'm invited over for dinner,' one of my customers told me, "I can hardly tell one place from another: I see the same Louis XV writing desk, the same Impressionist paintings on the walls, the same porcelain plaques on the furniture.'" To those who defy convention and repetition, the Frémontier gallery has all the attraction of the forbidden fruit. "People come here to some extent to feel like they are slumming it," explains "Jo." "Sometimes wives come without their husbands, then the couple become braver and eventually they take the plunge."

The Frémontiers, who never exhibit at outside exhibitions, devote all their efforts to the constantly changing decor of their three-floor showroom. Playing with Cordoba leather, Chinese wallpaper, and paneling by a follower of Pelagio Palagi, the decorator from Turin, they create contrasting backdrops for an astonishing array of chairs: late 18th-century Sicilian armchairs in the Chinese taste (Palazzina Cinese), a colonial cock-fighting chair in Macassar ebony and a mid-19th century music stool from the Palais Torlonia. "You will never find a Louis XV curved-back chair here." The same diversity exists in the other furniture: a pylon-shaped Egyptian cabinet, an Arte Povera closet, a Russian table made of porcelain and opaline, and a Spanish desk from the reign of Carlos IV. And wherever you look there are sophisticated objects, electroplates from the treasure of Ildesheim, Naples cast iron. "People don't come here to invest money or confirm their social status. What we offer our clients is, above all, astonishment, surprise, pleasure. An object must be pleasurable." What criteria do they use when choosing their stock? "When you're surprised, when you're not sure what something is, when

FRÉMONTIER
On the neogothic secretary of the 19th century, a big tankard and Renaissance mounted coconut, galvanoplasty of the 19th century.

FRÉMONTIER
Above: Khon-Hi China vase, flanked by a pair of Cordoba leather armchairs (Rio de Plata, 18th century).
Indo-Portoguese mirror of the 19th century. *Opposite:* Neo-Renaissance table by Lebois. *Bacchus* in white marble
by Ludovico Salvetti. Bust of *Julius Caesar,* Roman head of the 3rd century, draped clothes added in the 18th century.

you have no idea, but you know it's something good." You can definitely trust them on that score, and the two chairs in the Louvre's new 19th-century rooms, the table in the Corning Museum, and the bowls by Levillain and Barbedienne in the Musée d'Orsay prove that there is not only flair but serious knowledge behind the acquisitions.

It is understood, of course, that the 19th is their favorite century, especially French style with all its mixtures and stylistic hybrids, as well as European style in which the blending of influences and daring adaptations also create new, more exciting and provocative species. Their favorites are Charles de Beistegui, owner of the castle of Groussay, Peter Wilson at Clavary whom they discovered in the 1970s, and all those decorators who—like them—are convinced that an object can be transformed and recreated by the decor around it.

CLAUDINE GUÉRIN

Le Cabinet de Curiosité, 7ᵉ arr.

The store was once the local pharmacy, its many shelves lined with flasks, jars and pillboxes in the setting of neo-classical paneling interspersed with pilasters. In 1957, the pharmacist moved on and the antique dealer Jean Hébert took his place but the woodwork remained, an ideal setting for the oldtime display of curios in the Bonnier de la Mosson style: a disconcerting mix of objects from nature, scientific instruments, craftwork, botanical models, African masks, small bronzes and mounted nautilus shells. "When my husband and I began to hunt for antiques, we used to visit Jean Hébert regularly, because he never refused to give us information or an opinion. He was a scholar whose speciality was scientific instruments." Claudine and Jean-Claude Guérin each had a full-time job when they began antique-hunting "every other Saturday" alternating with a display at Paul Bert. They took the fateful step when the occasion arose to take over the curiosity shop. They set out to make it look spectacular, with crocodiles on the ceiling, large astronomical magnifying glasses and even a stuffed rhinoceros.

For the past eight years, Claudine has been running the curio shop on her own, gathering anything she considers to be unusual, from a Chardin-style bottle to a monkey skeleton, a carved peasant walking-cane to Polynesian hatchets, from the portrait of a child to a Murano glass figurine, from a bouquet of flowers to an ivory skull. This is a cabinet of curiosities which could have been assembled by an artist, a series of still lifes and vanity paintings with the things gleaned from chance meetings and encounters. Wooden mannequins, pedestals and easels re-inforce the impression of an attic-studio suitable for artistic reverie. A chandelier on the ceiling, a few items of furniture, charming paintings, and portraits of children and animals all contribute to the impression of a private room, which brings the store as many curious visitors as it does customers.

Covering curios as well as folk art, natural objects as well as scientific instruments, the *Cabinet de Curiosité* attracts many collectors with special interests, but Claudine Guérin refuses to concentrate on a single subject. "I never buy an object just to make a profit: it's more important that I like it, that it's of good quality and that it fits in with the other things that I have in stock. The most discriminating connoisseurs are sensitive to unique objects, such as this large wooden mannequin whose dress opens to reveal a closet. Sometimes, the collectors themselves inform me of the origins, traditional uses or history of an object."

The museums also appreciate Claudine Guérin's curios. The Getty Museum bought a "witch's mirror," a master-piece of craftsmanship whose polished surface is sprinkled with tiny mirrors that expand reflected space to include a profusion of disconcerting and unexpected microcosms. A symbol for the *Cabinet* on the Rue de Beaune and, obviously, for the curio in general: it's simply another way of looking at the things around us.

GUÉRIN

Above: Wooden and ivory statuettes, school of Simon Trogel (Tyrol, 18th c.). Carved and painted wooden female figure, its skirt opening onto a cupboard. Panel, *The Hawker on the Square* (Austria, 1847). Dummy head of larch wood (Queyras, 19th c.). The *papier-mâché* staghead is from the 18th century.
Opposite: Reliquary figure known as a "Bakota" (Gabon). Fana knife (Gabon). Comb from the Salomon Islands. Stilt stirrups from the Marquesas Islands, Yaka mask (Congo). Bowl for Kawa of the Fidji Islands. Wickerwork armor from the Gilbert Islands. Spears (Congo). A dresser table (Savoy, 19th c.).

JEAN-CLAUDE HUREAU

La Galerie des Laques, 6ᵉ arr.

"My mother was the one who decided to name the shop *Galerie des laques* (The Lacquer Gallery). It wasn't necessarily a good idea because I've concentrated mainly on 18th-century items, but the name's still there." And Jean-Claude Hureau is still there, too—on the street that used to contain no less than seventy antique dealers from the Carrefour de la Croix-Rouge to the Boulevard Montparnasse. It used to be like a village with its own colorful characters, such as Kagna, an excellent antique-hunter who loved to be rude to the customers, Eugène Orliange and Fauché, who lived in a small mansion with no heating which was lit by naked light bulbs hanging from the ceiling. "My mother opened the boutique when I was fifteen. She had an intuition that this would one day be my trade."

Jean-Claude Hureau studied at both the Académie Jullian and the École du Louvre, and decided to become an antique dealer. "I never touched a paintbrush again, but painting gave me 'an eye' and a certain feel that is perhaps more of a connoisseur's than a dealer's." And, in spite of what he says, lacquer has been one of his passions, a passion he shares with the *marchands merciers* of the past and the great collectors. "Victor Hugo would have been one of my best clients—maybe he would have bought a few items of lacquerware from my store in order to dismantle them and turn them into a chest of drawers or a desk or even a mantelpiece." He has oriental lacquerware originally made for export, European lacquerware, *vernis Martin.* His particular favorite is oriental-style lacquerware made for Western tastes: objects owned by Marie-Antoinette, Napoleon III *chinoiseries,* and the Coromandel screens of the 1920s which Coco Chanel adored. Another of his passions: European gilded wooden furniture, opulent Louis XIV picture frames, and the large, generously proportioned, heavily carved and rather fantastical consoles in Louis XV style.

Hureau is also particularly fond of sculpture, which explains his love of terra cotta "so spontaneous, so vibrant." "Sculpture is three-dimensional, palpable, more sensual. Renaissance sculpture is superb, but I am also very interested in Carrier-Belleuse." The latter being an artist whom Hureau presented at the 1994 Biennale.

Jean-Claude Hureau, who considers himself to be a connoisseur, in the sense of someone who loves objects, cannot resist an unusual piece of furniture, a collector's item which has particularly lovely proportions or makes original use of wood and veneers. In this, he feels a similarity with the re-inventors of classic taste of the 20th century, such as Charles de Beistegui or Emilio Terry, whose star-studded "astrologer's" furniture he acquired. Hureau is also an admirer of Jean-Pierre Hagnauer, "a great antique dealer and decorator" and Madeleine Castaing, the great discoverer of a light, exquisite 19th-century style thirty years before anyone else. Other important figures who influenced his beginnings include René Weiller, who was a businessman above all, always doing deals and selling a lot to the Americans, or Nicolas Landau, a scholarly man who would launch into an improvisation on his Steinway piano while telling you the story of a mounted nautilus shell, pillaged by the Swedes from the treasures of Rudolph II of Hapsburg and then stolen again by one of Napoleon's officers.

Jean-Claude Hureau is as voluble on the subject of antique dealers as he is on the subject of antiques. One of his favorite pieces is a box in Japanese lacquer which belonged to Cardinal Mazarin, bought and then sold again by William Beckford, which later became the property of the tenth Duke of Hamilton, and is now in the Victoria & Albert Museum in London. Without picking up anchor from the Left Bank, Jean-Claude Hureau found a new port on the Right Bank: as of May 2000, he opened a second shop on 6, Rue de Miromesnil, at the very address where Colette started a beauty shop in 1932.

HUREAU

In front of a Chinese lacquer screen of the 18th century, decorated with golden palaces on a black background, two white Japanese porcelain bottles decorated with Japanese lacquer placed on black and gilt lacquer stands (first half of the 19th century). The polychrome Chinese lacquer chest used to belong to the Duke of Talleyrand (18th century).

HUREAU

Above: On the Piedmontese wooden table in the foreground stand a pair of porcelain vases from the manufactory of the Duke of Orleans (late 18th century). Beside it a Louis XIV inkstand in Boulle marquetry. On the gilt wooden Louis XV console table, a collection of Chinese *cloisonné* vases from the 18th and 19th centuries. On the wall, a Chinese painting on silk with Japanese influence (1850-1900). *Opposite:* A Louis XVI ottoman, stamped by Séné and a Louis XI chair, stamped by Dupain are placed in front of a painted lacquer screen of the 18th century (Chinese production for the European market).

GUY LADRIÈRE

Charles Ratton & Guy Ladrière, 7ᵉ arr. et 8ᵉ arr.

From the beginning, Ladrière had a huge appetite for looking, touching, understanding. Guy Ladrière is a sensual man, full of curiousity since his childhood when he served as an altar boy in a little church at Nogent-sur-Oise. "The church was half-romanesque and half-gothic, with sculptures, terra cotta figures–all you had to do was look. I acquired an eye then developed it."

His first job was as a haulier in Les Halles wholesale food market. Following someone's move, he was left with a number of unclaimed objects and that is how he got started. He would go antique-hunting in Province, knocking door to door or trading with dealers. When the Les Halles market moved from the center of Paris to the southern suburb of Rungis, he chose instead to open a booth at the flea market. This is when he made his first exciting finds as well as his first mistakes, but he was learning all the time. "I sold iron beds, chimney plaques, anything that was saleable, but I kept the best things for myself."

A choirboy's nostalgia? The discovery of a few relics from the Spitzer collection–enamels and earthenware–gave him a taste for medieval objects. "When I heard about Spitzer, I went to see and bought a copy of the illustrated catalog." He discovered a long line of heroes whose names were Revoil, Debruges, Soltykoff, and Carrand who, over a century and a half, had passed on the tradition of "high curiosity." The line lives on in unique 20th-century personalities such as Nicolas Landau or Michel Meyer Senior, "Who was a great guy, he was interested in everything, from scrap iron to glassware and mathematical objects. He knew about so many things, and I learned a lot from him." His greatest teacher was Charles Ratton, who added primitive art to the field of High Curiosity (Ratton could claim Helena Rubinstein as one of his clients) and who took part in the modern adventure by organizing the first exhibition of Surrealist items in his gallery on the Rue de Marignan. The acclaimed expert and the young dealer developed a bond and now Guy Ladrière carries on tradition as the head of the Ratton-Ladrière Gallery. "I carried on in all the fields in which he was interested, but imperceptibly I slid from the Middle Ages to the 17th, 18th and even the 19th centuries."

His gallery on the Quai Voltaire is full of sculptures: ivory virgins, mannerist bronzes, 18th-century terra cotta busts, competition entries. "This is the area with which I feel most comfortable and in which you can still make some real finds. Sculpture has not yet reached its full price, whereas I can only afford to buy a few items of primitive art per year." Guy Ladrière also invested in paintings, large and difficult works, from medieval illumination to mythological allegory, for museums and serious connoisseurs. There isn't much in the way of furniture, but you don't come to Ladrière to find furniture. He is surrounded by a team of collaborators who help him with documentation and sales, but he knows that nothing can take the place of experience in the field: at exhibitions, at the Hôtel Drouot auction house, everywhere.

"You need to know how to buy publicly, in front of everyone, something that does not exist, that cannot possibly exist, such as a Dürer drawing for six thousand francs or a large antique bronze. You need to go to lectures and symposia, read books, or spend three hours in a museum. Most people visit the museum once they've found something, personally, I go in search of something. Knowledge is the key–you need to know more than anyone else. But you need dreams as well. You need to use your imagination when you're confronted with something unknown and, above all, you have to see things through to the end."

LADRIÈRE
In the foreground, in front of an Italian wardrobe of the 17th century, a 16th-century German sculpture representing Saint Florian. In the passage leading to the study, on the floor, a relief typical of the Maître au chat, forger of the 19th century. Above, a painting by Bronzino from the Salviati collection, a Venetian marble of the 16th century showing *The Three Graces, Saint John the Baptist* by Nino Pisano and a *Portrait of a woman* by Cesare Dandini.

LADRIÈRE

Above: In front of a painting of the French neoclassical school, a marble head by Tullio Lombardo, an Etruscan perfume-burner,
a Roman bronze of the 17th century representing Charles II of Spain, from the collection of the Marquis del Carpio and the Dukes of Alba,
bronze *River God* by Michel Anguier, and a bronze Roman sculpted portrait representing Polydeukes, a friend of the emperor Lucius Verus.
Opposite: A Suku mask (Zaire) is laying on a sculpted portrait of the Emperor Vespasian.

FRANK LAIGNEAU

Galerie Frank Laigneau, 7ᵉ arr.

"When I learned that this bookshop was for rent, I didn't hesitate–it's on the street where I grew up," explains Frank Laigneau who first settled Rue Bellechasse. There is still something in this young antique dealer like the tenacity of a child who knows what he wants and fights to get it. He has the physique of a Prince Charming and the qualities of "projection," which first came in handy for his budding career as an actor–he performed with Danielle Darrieux and Jean-Pierre Aumont and in a movie about the life of Joseph Conrad. After five years as an actor, he changed his course: he studied psychology and architecture at the university then took art history courses at the École du Louvre. To make some money, he and a friend, Patrick Hourcade, designed a set of furniture in slate and metal that was produced in a limited stamped edition, and exhibited at Gladys Mougin, where it met with critical if not popular success. Laigneau then became a broker for several important dealers, such as Alain Demachy.

His first revelation: René Herbst, the contents of whose work-shop he found and presented at his first *Pavillon des Antiquaires.* What he liked in this precursor was the austerity of line, the design, but it was necessary to convince the customers. "Tubular furniture had gone out of style since it had been rediscovered in the 1970s. I located and displayed only the pieces from the very brief period of glory around 1930, took care to separate the innovators from the followers, reminded clients that the furniture they saw in beige canvas used to be covered in foalskin, leather and Burckhalter tapestry, and that it used to be in such luxurious surroundings as Tamara de Lempicka's studio, the villa of de Noailles, or the palace of the Maharajah of Indore." Laigneau's other passion is the 19th century, which he considers to be "less expensive and less intimidating than the 18th century; there are still plenty of discoveries to be made."

His museums of reference are Orsay and Compiègne, which contains masterpieces purchased by the Empress Eugenie at the World Fairs, such as the limewood piece by Giroux whose treelike aspect already seems to announce Art Nouveau. "It was an era of deviation, excess, folly, and inconsistencies, where you need to understand its rules, proportions, and subtleties." Of these follies, taste for the Japanese-style seems to him the most intriguing. He acquired this enthusiasm from the collector, Roberto Polo, who converted to the 19th century after having amassed a remarkable 18th-century collection fifteen years previously. He is particularly interested in the best examples of French cabinet-making, but is not insensitive to an end table created by the Swedish designer Horrström who studied in Paris at the same time as Larsonn and who expertly combines traditional Nordic hammered brass and Japanese-style elements.

In contrast to this extravagance, he also takes an interest in those British esthetic movements which have combined the oriental and the western styles, such as Anglo-Japanese *à la* Godwin. Here is an ormolu bust by Clésinger, there a table by Diehl with a porcelain base, a ceramic by Herbst, and a neo-Renaissance French pedestal table. With the agility of a gymnast, Frank Laigneau manages to maintain a happy balance in his new gallery, 8, Rue de Miromesnil, between showcase items and monumental furniture, international purism and eclectic flights of fancy. In the strict decor, every object has its place and keeps its distance, leaving the visitor the opportunity of consciously succumbing to its charms.

LAIGNEAU

On the center table created by Gio Ponti (circa 1940), an African-style glazed terra cotta head, signed S. Ghysbrecht (dated 1928). On the pair of mahogony columns stamped Jacob (circa 1840), two glazed terra cotta vases (France, circa 1930).

PHILIPPE LA QUERRIERE

Thenadey, Philippe La Querrière, 7e arr.

"I must have fallen into a magic caldron when I was little, because I always loved old objects. I used to bike over to the "vendues," as they called the auctions in my part of the world, and I'd come back with a stack of six or seven chairs." Law studies to please his family did nothing to dull Philippe La Querrière's enthusiasm, and he began to hunt for certain dealers, such as Madame Robert, who had a store on the corner of the Rue de Beaune and the Rue de Verneuil. In 1968, the opportunity presented itself to acquire the store, and Madame Robert stayed on as saleswoman.

La Querrière specializes in items which would have been acquired on the "Grand Tour:" obelisks and columns, busts, tables inlaid with pietra dura, boxes with intaglio moldings, views of Rome and Napolitan gouache paintings, models of monuments in cork and mahogany, drawings of ornaments and architecture. The mixture of rigor and charm delights decorators such as Serge Royaux and François Catroux. "It was the era when Americans were interested in large architectural drawings in the Beaux-Arts style. I remember sending some of them to the School of the same name, and the first exhibition on the Beaux-Arts tradition was held in New York." Philippe La Querrière subsequently expanded his operation. He had always coveted the Thénadey sign on the corner of the Quai Voltaire and the Rue des Saints-Pères: "Germaine Thenadey and her brother Maurice were the fourth generation of antique dealers, who had begun as tapestry-makers in the 18th century. They lived in the mezzanine above the shop and displayed high-quality but not very exciting merchandise, what I would call 'Parisian provincial.' He would go to the Drouot auctions and re-upholster chairs in the evening. She ran the shop with the majesty of the cashier at a fancy pastry shop: she wore her hair tied back in a bun, so that she looked like something from an 18th-century glass painting."

The Thenadey's gallery has been left as it was: its creaky floorboards, soot-blackened ceilings, and walls covered with tattered fabric would have pleased Philippe Jullian. "When a fabric gets too worn, I merely cover it over with another," explains the antique dealer who very well the atmosphere just wouldn't be the same after a thorough cleaning. In the big window on the quay, only a Turkish 18th century drawing room has been installed; on the ceiling, a 17th century silk bedspread—we're at Vicotr Hugo's Hauteville House. "It's a timeless background, the objects look natural in it, they don't seem like intruders." From the beginning, when he opened in 1976, Philippe La Querrière offered old fabrics and braided trimmings, launching a Visconti-style fashion. "New York decorators chartered small aircraft to bring over early examples of button upholstery." His love of old fabrics led La Querrière to reissue them, and he took over the name and premises of *Comoglio* on Rue Jacob. Philippe La Querrière's specialty is simple but expensive objects such as a Louis XIII pen-holder, a Louis XIV washstand, Louis XVI morocco leather bellows, a Charles X romantic "cathedral-style" jam jar, a nutcracker as handsome as a surgical instrument, birdcages, an embroidered nightcap on a wooden candlestick for Voltaire, a few Empire ivory-and-mahogany chests, the whole looking like a still-life by Chardin or Fantin-Latour. It all seems as if, at any moment, a ghost from a Turkish scene by Liotard will float down the grand staircase.

LA QUERRIÈRE

Opposite: In the yellow drawing room. A gilt wooden Louis XVI table with a silk brocade top. On it, a multi-layered catch-all decorated with entangled vines.

(following pages)
LA QUERRIÈRE

Left: In the green drawing room, a set of paintings from the atelier of Fontaine and, on the pedestal table, a bust of *Rose* by Rodin.
Right: Two Chinese lacquered terra cotta figures, late 17th century.

ALAIN MOATTI

Moatti, 6ᵉ arr.

"I don't believe it! Yet another specialist in the unsaleable," exclaimed Nicolas Landau in the 1960s when he discovered the little boutique newly opened by Alain Moatti and his wife Michèle on the Rue de la Huchette. Both were young students, recent graduates of the École du Louvre.

Apart from a grandfather who was a jeweler and who introduced his grandson to antique jewelry, nothing predestined Alain Moatti for the trade. He was not born into a family of antique dealers, but was admitted to the clique by Nicolas Landau and Michel Meyer. "Nicolas Landau had come from central Europe, a cultivated dealer who had discovered and re-introduced the fashion for cabinets of curiosities. For him, objects were not seen in isolation but were elements of a style, an era. He knew how to tie them in with decoration, architecture, and painting. Michel Meyer was like a character out of a novel by Balzac—setting didn't matter to him. He lived very modestly but was passionate about art objects. He was so radiant that things gravitated towards him. Wherever he was, people would come to show him artefacts, and all the biggest dealers would come to see his latest finds."

In 1967, Alain and Michèle Moatti opened their store on the Rue des Saints-Pères, at a time when Saint-Germain-des-Prés had not yet been invaded by clothes. A room on the ground floor was converted into a studiolo thanks to Renaissance paneling decorated with marquetry scenes in false perspective. There was no other furniture, except for a table edged with a valance on which a few bronzes were arranged. Behind the woodwork paneling which had been turned into a cabinet, there were a few ivories, pieces of amber, mounted gemstones and gold and silver pieces. The first floor housed the bigger objects: marble statues, large bronzes, a few precious fabrics arranged on a chest, a cabinet reserved for drawings. There were a few paintings, consisting of mysteriously symbolic still lifes and large allegories, no facile subjects. No one comes to Alain Moatti to furnish a home or decorate a wall. Only an intiated few were allowed upstairs: his accomplices or collectors, museum curators, and other dealers.

"I rarely sell anything 'decorative,' something that would look well in a carefully designed interior. Most of my clients love the objects for themselves." The paneling on the ground floor unmistakably sets the tone: Alain Moatti is a Renaissance humanist. His bible is Julius von Schlosser's "Cabinet of Curiosities," his tutelary parents are Rudolph II and Isabella d'Este, his favorite museums the Victoria and Albert in London and the Kunsthistorisches Museum in Vienna. He loves the marvellous, the strange, the rare, and has a predilection for bronze, waxing lyrical whenever he mentions the bust of Cosmo de Medici by Cellini in the Bargello in Florence, which he visits regularly. But he also loves fragile materials such as glass to which he owes his first successful transactions.

His clientele has changed over the years. The polite scholars who spent their Saturday afternoons on the Rue des Saints-Pères twenty years ago have given way to the international jet-set who would just as soon buy large modern paintings as neo-classical terra cotta relief as quality bronzes and intend "to live with them" in their environment. The desire to collect complementary sets of objects has been replaced by a certain eclecticism based more in taste than in knowledge. Few traditional decorators visit Alain Moatti. Only someone such as François Joseph Graf, who is in the know, can share with his clients a knowledgeable and flamboyant approach to objects. One of the joys of a great antique dealer is to rediscover the object he originally acquired in the dusty obscurity of a provincial saleroom now basking under the spotlights of a museum—Alain Moatti has had the pleasure with the *Apollo* by Adrien de Vries, which is currently in the Getty Museum.

MOATTI
A collection of music instruments from the 16th to the 18th century, waiting to be hung. On the pedestal, a terra cotta *Saint John the Baptist* by Jacopo Sansovino, early 17th century.

MOATTI

Above: Taddeo Landini, *Crowned Siren* (detail of a monumental bronze, Rome, 16th century).
Some examples of German medals of the 16th century. A bronze *Ariane* by Michel Anguier (detail,
France, late 17th century). *Opposite:* In front of the Renaissance studiolo, a marble *Apollo* by Pierre Legros
(circa 1700). *Following pages:* Under the grisaille *modello* by Francesco Monti (Bologna, second half
of the 18th century), *Pluto capturing Proserpina,* a bronze by G. B. Foggini (Florence, circa 1700),
stands on a table covered with red draperies. In the center, on a column, *David,* a marble statue
from the studio of Alessandro Vittoria (Venice, 1603). On the armchair, a Venetian ivory guitar (1656).
On the floor, a pair of globes on stands with black and gold wooden feet (Berlin, 1780).

THE
MARCHÉ AUX PUCES

For a long time, the Marché aux Puces (flea market) at Saint-Ouen, on the outskirts of Paris, was a paradise for antique-hunters who could spot an Urbino majolica amongst what the ordinary customer took to be provincial pottery, and where a Renaissance bronze was less appreciated than a piece by Barbedienne. You could even still find a few "period pieces" (the period in question being the 18th century) amidst the Louis-Philippe secretaries and console tables. Today, the important deals are done at dawn and the precious objects whisked away to more prestigious settings. What remains are charming and unusual wares which are the sort of thing also to be found in the Carré Rive Gauche.

For lovers of the picturesque, the Vernaison Market has retained the charm of the old, unpretentious Marché aux Puces. Biron, however, remains faithful to the Faubourg Saint-Antoine with its shiny bronzes, Jules-Vallès always gives the impression that there are wonderful finds to be made, but the real action is at Serpette and Paul-Bert, essential stops on the route taken by antique-hunters and casual strollers alike.

The best flea market booths cunningly combine old industrial shelves, decorative paintings, birdcages, tin signs, garage lamps, painted console-tables, and large plasterwork statues to create a cabinet of outsized and decorative curiosities for people wanting to furnish apartments in the fashionable 16th arrondissement or manor houses in Provence. A few booths will also display unusual objects, small bronzes, or drawings. Every flea market genre has its specialists: for example, wooden country furniture, lace, enameled advertising signs, posters, Vuitton luggage, postcards, fountain pens, dishes from cafés, dolls, and so on, but the main quality and function of Serpette and Paul-Bert is to serve as a stepping-stone on the career path of most antique dealers who, in successive waves, create tomorrow's market for antiques.

As early as the 1960s, dealers would scour the Marché aux Puces picking up "antique" junk for "next-to-nothing" on Saturday mornings, and resell it on Saturday afternoons. In the hustle and bustle of unpacking, these new objects, which are still anonymous, are bought on a whim, purely for their unusual aspect or their good condition; only afterwards are discoveries and attributions made. Art Nouveau was followed by Art Deco, then came the rage for 1930s and 1940s objects. Today, plastic beds designed by Marc Held and sold at Prisunic may feature next to the most recent mass-produced chairs by Starck. Chairs designed by Piano and Lord Rogers for the library of the Pompidou Center have replaced the Privilège armchairs designed by Garouste and Bonetti. The objects found at the Marché aux Puces emerge as the next antiques for a new market. This is where used and rejected furniture, whose accumulated dirt has not yet acquired the attractions of a patina, eventually ends up. It is snatched up by the quickest and sharpest hunters and dispatched to their warehouses, before it resurfaces some time later in new showrooms, which were once in Saint-Germain-des-Prés but are now in the Bastille and Belleville.

The Marché aux Puces is the school of hard knocks through which many antique dealers have passed. Deals are done swiftly, stock moves fast. Reflexes are forged in the fever of Saturday mornings and even more so on Fridays. Not all of the most successful booth-owners move on, however: some remain faithful to their pitch and have even chosen to live nearby in the little millstone and tile houses where objects can be displayed as they would be shown in decorating magazines. There is even something of a return to the Marché aux Puces among certain dealers, who retain their store "in town" but find a different customer base in Saint-Ouen, and who enjoy the warm, friendly atmosphere.

Preceding page: **DE TEMPS EN TEMPS** "Rustic Louis XIII" chairs, Restauration-period barber's stand. In the background, a Leda allegory in a screen's medallion. *Above:* **OLIVIER DEBOSCKER** 1960's black lacquered Danish chair, against a decorative painted panel by Grelot (1984). *Opposite:* **RACT-MADOUX** In the foreground, close-up of part of the *Nessa* lamp (model produced by Artémide starting in 1965), yellow plastic. Lip-shaped sofa by Studoi (1965). On the wall, a painting by G. Trinquier (1972).

Above: **RACT-MADOUX** In front of a piece of furniture by Guermonprez (1955), a chair by Harry Bertoia with its original red cover. Murano glass ceiling lamp by Gino Vistosi. *Opposite:* **PIERRE BAZALGUES** On a 1940's cabinet sheathed in red leather, an anatomical model (Holland?) by Van E. Petouvio and a cardboard horse head by doctor Auzoux (late 19th century). In the background, a 19th-century copy of an 18th-century portrait.

APPENDICES

ANNE-SOPHIE DUVAL

JEAN-PAUL AND MICHEL FABRE

FRANÇOIS FABIUS

NICOLE ALTÉRO

Addresses

Classics

DIDIER AARON & CIE
118, rue du Faubourg-Saint-Honoré
75008 Paris
Tel.: 01 47 42 47 34   Fax: 01 42 66 24 17

AVELINE
94, rue du Faubourg-Saint-Honoré,
place Beauvau, 75008 Paris
Tel.: 01 42 66 60 29   Fax: 01 42 66 45 91

EUGÈNE BECKER
136, rue du Faubourg-Saint-Honoré
75008 Paris
Tel.: 01 42 89 44 90   Fax: 01 42 89 44 91

ARIANE DANDOIS
92, rue du Faubourg-Saint-Honoré
75008 Paris
Tel.: 01 43 12 39 39   Fax: 01 43 12 39 29

FABIUS FRÈRES
152, boulevard Haussmann
75008 Paris
Tel.: 01 45 62 39 18   Fax: 01 45 62 53 07

FABRE ET FILS
19, rue Balzac 75008 Paris
Tel.: 01 45 61 17 52   Fax: 01 43 59 03 97

GISMONDI
20, rue Royale
75008 Paris
Tel.: 01 42 60 73 89   Fax: 01 42 60 98 94
Les Remparts
06600 Antibes
Tel.: 04 93 34 06 67   Fax: 04 93 34 35 84

MARCEL GRUNSPAN
6 and 8, rue Royale 75008 Paris
Tel.: 01 42 60 57 57   Fax: 01 40 20 95 50

KRAEMER ET CIE
43, rue de Monceau 75008 Paris
Tel.: 01 45 63 31 23   Fax: 01 45 63 54 36

J. KUGEL
279, rue Saint-Honoré 75008 Paris
Tel.: 01 42 60 86 23   Fax: 01 42 61 06 72

FRANÇOIS LÉAGE
178, rue du Faubourg-Saint-Honoré
75008 Paris
Tel.: 01 45 63 43 46   Fax: 01 42 56 46 30

ÉTIENNE LÉVY
42, rue de Varenne
75007 Paris
Tel.: 01 45 44 65 50   Fax: 01 45 49 05 38

JEAN LUPU
43, rue du Faubourg-Saint-Honoré
75008 Paris
Tel.: 01 42 65 93 19   Fax: 01 42 65 49 16

MICHEL MEYER
24, avenue Matignon
75008 Paris
Tel.: 01 42 66 62 95   Fax: 01 49 24 07 88

YVES MIKAELOFF
10, rue Royale 75008 Paris
Tel.: 01 42 61 64 42   Fax: 01 49 27 07 32

PERRIN ANTIQUAIRES
98 and 178 rue du Faubourg-Saint-Honoré
75008 Paris
Tel.: 01 42 65 01 38 / 01 40 76 07 76
Fax: 01 49 24 04 08 / 01 40 76 09 37

PHILIPPE PERRIN
3, quai Voltaire 75007 Paris
Tel.: 01 42 60 27 20   Fax: 01 42 61 32 61

SEGOURA
14, place François-Ier 75008 Paris
Tel.: 01 42 89 20 20   Fax: 01 42 89 64 13

BERNARD STEINITZ
9, rue du Cirque
75008 Paris
Tel.: 01 42 89 40 50   Fax: 01 42 89 40 60

Moderns

ALB ANTIQUITÉS
3, rue de Lille 75007 Paris
Tel.: 01 47 03 45 58   Fax: 01 47 03 07 37

ÉRIC ALLART
5, rue de Beaune 75007 Paris
Tel.: 01 42 61 31 44   Fax: 01 42 61 32 10

L'ARC-EN-SEINE
27 and 31, rue de Seine
75006 Paris
Tel.: 01 43 29 11 02   Fax: 01 43 29 97 66

ALEXANDRE BIAGGI
14, rue de Seine 75006 Paris
Tel.: 01 44 07 34 73   Fax: 01 44 07 34 52

GALERIE CHASTEL-MARÉCHAL
5, rue Bonaparte 75006 Paris
Tel.: 01 40 46 82 61   Fax: 01 43 26 24 47

JEAN-LOUIS DANANT
36, avenue Matignon 75008 Paris
Tel.: 01 42 89 40 15   Fax: 01 42 89 40 10

M. DANBON-J. POKORNY
25, rue de Lille 75007 Paris
Tel.: 01 40 20 01 79   Fax: 01 49 27 07 94

LUC DEBRUILLE
3, rue de Lille 75007 Paris
Tel./Fax: 01 42 61 78 72

STÉPHANE DESCHAMPS
19, rue Guénégaud 75006 Paris
Tel./Fax: 01 46 33 58 00

DENIS DORIA
16, rue de Seine 75006 Paris
Tel.: 01 43 54 73 49   Fax: 01 43 25 68 72

GALERIE DOWN TOWN
33, rue de Seine 75006 Paris
Tel.: 01 46 33 82 41   Fax: 01 43 29 10 75

JEAN-FRANÇOIS DUBOIS
15, rue de Lille 75007 Paris
Tel.: 01 42 60 40 17   Fax: 01 42 96 04 24

GALERIE JEAN-JACQUES DUTKO
13, rue Bonaparte 75006 Paris
Tel.: 01 43 26 96 13   Fax: 01 43 29 21 91

ANNE-SOPHIE DUVAL
5, quai Malaquais 75006 Paris
Tel.: 01 43 54 51 16   Fax: 01 40 46 95 12

GALERIE PATRICK FOURTIN
9, rue des Bons-Enfants 75001 Paris
Tel.: 01 42 60 12 63   Fax: 01 42 60 19 63

GALERIE YVES GASTOU
12, rue Bonaparte 75006 Paris
Tel.: 01 53 73 00 10   Fax: 01 53 73 00 12

GALERIE JOUSSE-SEGUIN
34, rue de Charonne
and 5, rue des Taillandiers
75011 Paris
Tel.: 01 47 00 32 35   Fax: 01 40 21 82 95

GALERIE JACQUES LACOSTE
22, rue de Lille 75007 Paris
Tel.: 01 40 20 81 82   Fax: 01 40 53 85 19

ANNE LAJOIX
16, rue des Saints-Pères 75007 Paris
Tel.: 01 42 86 90 94   Fax: 01 42 86 90 96

FÉLIX MARCILHAC
8, rue Bonaparte 75006 Paris
Tel.: 01 43 26 47 36   Fax: 01 43 54 96 87

JOËLLE MORTIER-VALAT
13, rue des Saints-Pères
75007 Paris
Tel.: 01 42 60 28 30   Fax: 01 42 60 28 16

JEAN-PIERRE ORINEL
12, rue de Lille 75007 Paris
Tel.: 01 42 97 58 66   Fax: 01 42 97 58 67

EUGÈNE BECKER

JACQUES LACOSTE

CLAUDINE GUÉRIN

BOB AND CHESKA VALLOIS

GALERIE DU PASSAGE
20-22, galerie Véro-Dodat 75001 Paris
Tel.: 01 42 36 01 13   Fax: 01 40 41 98 86

GALERIE ÉRIC PHILIPPE
25, galerie Véro-Dodat 75001 Paris
Tel.: 01 42 33 28 26   Fax: 01 42 21 17 93

GALERIE PLAISANCE
3, rue Bonaparte 75006 Paris
Tel./Fax: 01 43 29 05 38

MAROUN H. SALLOUM
17 bis, quai Voltaire and 6, rue de Lille
75007 Paris
Tel.: 01 40 15 95 01   Fax: 01 49 27 09 84

PATRICK SERRAIRE
30, rue de Lille 75007 Paris
Tel.: 01 47 03 43 13

VALLOIS
41, rue de Seine 75006 Paris
Tel.: 01 43 29 50 84   Fax: 01 43 29 90 73

JACQUES DE VOS
7, rue Bonaparte 75006 Paris
Tel.: 01 43 29 88 94   Fax: 01 40 46 95 45

GALERIE OLIVIER WATELET
11, rue Bonaparte 75006 Paris
Tel.: 01 43 26 07 87   Fax: 01 43 25 99 33

Curiosity

AKKO VAN ACKER
3, rue de l'Université 75007 Paris
Tel.: 01 42 60 22 03   Fax: 01 42 60 46 87

GALERIE ALAIN & GÉRARD
5 and 7, rue de Beaune
75007 Paris
Tel.: 01 42 61 23 95   Fax: 01 40 20 01 92

GALERIE ALTÉRO
21, quai Voltaire 75007 Paris
Tel.: 01 42 61 19 90   Fax: 01 40 20 03 30

ARABESQUE
8, rue de Commaille 75008 Paris
Tel./Fax: 01 45 49 35 54

GALERIE B.J.F.
27, rue de Verneuil 75007 Paris
Tel.: 01 42 61 36 46   Fax: 01 42 61 22 00

FRANÇOIS ET DOMINIQUE BIANCARELLI
19, rue de Beaune 75007 Paris
Tel.: 01 42 61 23 05   Fax: 01 42 61 24 55

JEAN-FRANÇOIS DE BLANCHETTI
2, rue des Saints-Pères
75007 Paris
Tel.: 01 42 60 22 43   Fax: 01 42 96 23 47

LUC BOUVERET
7, quai Voltaire 75007 Paris
Tel.: 01 40 20 91 21   Fax: 01 40 20 91 31

LE CABINET DE CURIOSITÉ
23, rue de Beaune 75007 Paris
Tel./Fax: 01 42 61 09 57

GALERIE CAMOIN ANTIQUITÉS
9, quai Voltaire 75007 Paris
Tel.: 01 42 61 82 06   Fax: 01 42 61 24 09

CHOLLET-VUAILLAT
44, rue de Lille 75007 Paris
Tel./Fax: 01 42 61 28 08

DENIS DERVIEUX
25, rue de Beaune 75007 Paris
Tel./Fax: 01 40 15 99 20

ANTONY EMBDEN
15, quai Voltaire 75007 Paris
Tel.: 01 42 61 04 06   Fax: 01 42 61 40 89

FLORE
6, rue de Beaune 75007 Paris
Tel.: 01 42 61 42 22   Fax: 01 42 61 42 32

FRÉMONTIER
5, quai Voltaire 75007 Paris
Tel.: 01 42 61 64 90   Fax: 01 42 61 04 96

GOSSELIN-DUBREUIL
6, rue de Beaune 75007 Paris
Tel./Fax: 01 42 61 35 58

H. P. ANTIQUITÉS-LE STUDIO
1, rue Allent 75007 Paris
Tel.: 01 40 20 00 56   Fax: 01 45 35 44 54

GALERIE SANDRINE LADRIÈRE
3, rue de l'Université 75007 Paris
Tel.: 01 42 61 53 01   Fax: 01 42 60 08 03

GALERIE FRANK LAIGNEAU
8, rue de Miromesnil 75008 Paris
Tel.: 06 11 85 02 97

PHILIPPE LA QUERRIÈRE
27, rue de Beaune 75007 Paris
Tel.: 01 42 61 00 84

LA GALERIE DES LAQUES
74, rue du Cherche-Midi 75006 Paris
Tel.: 01 45 48 88 82   Fax: 01 45 44 31 81
6, rue Miromesnil 75008 Paris
Tel.: 01 40 07 08 37   Fax: 01 40 07 08 29

ÉDOUARD DE LA MARQUE
2, rue des Saints-Pères
75007 Paris
Tel./Fax: 01 42 60 71 62

JEAN-LUC MÉCHICHE
182, rue du Faubourg-Saint-Honoré
75008 Paris
Tel.: 01 45 63 20 11   Fax: 01 42 25 91 34

MOATTI
77, rue des Saints-Pères
75006 Paris
Tel.: 01 42 22 91 04   Fax: 01 45 44 86 17

GÉRARD MONLUC
7, rue de l'Université 75007 Paris
Tel.: 01 42 96 18 19   Fax: 01 42 60 20 51

NICOLE MUGLER
2, rue de l'Université 75007 Paris
Tel./Fax: 01 42 96 36 45

PHILIPPE MURAT-DAVID
3, rue de Beaune 75007 Paris
Tel./Fax: 01 42 61 64 53

MICHEL OTTIN
33, quai Voltaire 75007 Paris
Tel.: 01 42 61 19 88   Fax: 01 42 61 32 41

GALERIE PERPITCH
240, boulevard Saint-Germain
75007 Paris
Tel.: 01 45 48 37 67   Fax: 01 42 84 04 64

CHARLES RATTON & GUY LADRIÈRE
11, quai Voltaire 75007 Paris
Tel.: 01 42 61 29 79   Fax: 01 42 56 00 72
14, rue de Marignan 75008 Paris
Tel.: 01 43 59 58 21   Fax: 01 42 56 00 72

MARC RÉVILLON D'APREVAL
23, quai Voltaire
75007 Paris
Tel.: 01 42 61 27 36   Fax: 01 42 61 43 70

THENADEY
1, quai Voltaire 75007 Paris
Tel.: 01 42 60 77 33   Fax: 01 40 51 70 56

Specialties

African art
GALERIE ALAIN DE MONBRISON
2, rue des Beaux-Arts
75006 Paris
Tel.: 01 46 34 05 20   Fax: 01 46 34 67 25

GALERIE RATTON-HOURDÉ
10, rue des Beaux-Arts
75006 Paris
Tel.: 01 46 33 32 02   Fax: 01 46 33 34 02

Ceramics
LEFEBVRE ET FILS ANTIQUITÉS
24, rue du Bac 75007 Paris
Tel.: 01 42 61 18 40   Fax: 01 42 86 91 58

MICHEL VANDERMEERSCH
21, quai Voltaire 75007 Paris
Tel.: 01 42 61 23 10   Fax: 01 49 27 98 49

GUY LADRIÈRE FRANCK LAIGNEAU MATTHIEU DE PRÉMONT AND OLIVIER WATELET FRANÇOIS LAFFANOUR

Classical archaeology
GALERIE SERRES
15, rue Bonaparte 75006 Paris
Tel.: 01 43 25 78 27 Fax: 01 46 33 55 32
GALERIE URAEUS
24, rue de Seine 75006 Paris
Tel.: 01 43 26 91 31

Drawings
GALERIE DE BAYSER
69, rue Sainte-Anne 75002 Paris
Tel.: 01 47 03 49 87 Fax: 01 42 97 51 03

Empire, militaria
LE SPHINX
104, rue du Faubourg-Saint-Honoré
75008 Paris
Tel.: 01 42 65 90 96 Fax: 01 42 65 90 97

English furniture
ANDRÉE HIGGINS & CIE
52-54, rue de l'Université
75007 Paris
Tel.: 01 45 48 75 28 Fax: 01 45 48 07 98

Gold, silver
AU VIEUX PARIS
4, rue de la Paix 75002 Paris
Tel.: 01 42 61 00 89 Fax: 01 42 61 38 65
ÉDOUARD DE SÉVIN
Louvre des Antiquaires
2, place du Palais-Royal 75001 Paris
Tel.: 01 42 61 57 99 Fax: 01 47 03 32 07

Middle Ages, Renaissance
ANTIQUITÉS BRESSET & FILS
197, boulevard Saint-Germain 75007 Paris
Tel.: 01 45 48 18 24 Fax: 01 42 60 59 38
5, quai Voltaire 75007 Paris
Tel.: 01 42 60 78 13 Fax: 01 42 60 59 38
BRIMO DE LAROUSSILHE
7, quai Voltaire 75007 Paris
Tel.: 01 42 60 74 76 Fax: 01 42 60 53 92

Modern paintings, Japanese prints
GALERIE BERES
25, quai Voltaire 75007 Paris
Tel.: 01 42 61 27 91 Fax: 01 49 27 95 88

Oriental art
JACQUES BARRÈRE
36, rue Mazarine 75006 Paris
Tel.: 01 43 26 57 61 Fax: 01 46 34 02 83
CHRISTIAN DEYDIER
21, rue du Bac 75007 Paris
Tel.: 01 40 20 97 34 Fax: 01 40 20 97 39
GÉRARD-LÉVY
17, rue de Beaune 75007 Paris
Tel.: 01 42 61 26 55 Fax: 01 42 96 03 91
C.T. LOO ET CIE
48, rue de Courcelles 75008 Paris
Tel.: 01 45 62 53 15 Fax: 01 45 62 07 02
MYRNA MYERS
11, rue de Beaune 75007 Paris
Tel.: 01 42 61 11 08 Fax: 01 30 82 49 17

Porcelains
DRAGESCO-CRAMOISAN
13, rue de Beaune
75007 Paris
Tel.: 01 42 61 18 20 Fax: 01 42 85 40 37

Russian art
GOLOVANOFF
21, rue de Beaune
75007 Paris
Tel.: 01 42 61 03 75 Fax: 01 42 61 12 99
PETROUCHKA
18, rue de Beaune
75007 Paris
Tel.: 01 42 61 66 65 Fax: 01 42 61 06 53

Scientific documents and instruments
LIBRAIRIE ALAIN BRIEUX
48, rue Jacob 75006 Paris
Tel.: 01 42 60 21 98 Fax: 01 42 60 55 24

Sculpture
PATRICE BELLANGER
198, boulevard Saint-Germain
75007 Paris
Tel.: 01 45 44 19 15 Fax: 01 42 84 02 29

Tapestry
GALERIE CHEVALIER
17, quai Voltaire 75007 Paris
Tel.: 01 42 60 72 68 Fax: 01 42 86 99 06

Tapestry, Renaissance
GALERIE BLONDEEL-DEROYAN
11, rue de Lille 75007 Paris
Tel.: 01 49 27 96 22 Fax: 01 49 27 96 18

19th-century paintings
ANDRÉ LEMAIRE
43, rue de Verneuil
75007 Paris
Tel./Fax: 01 42 61 12 55

19th-century paintings and drawings
GALERIE JACQUES FISCHER
46, rue de Verneuil
75007 Paris
Tel.: 01 42 61 17 82 Fax: 01 42 60 13 37
GALERIE GREINER
14, galerie Véro-Dodat
75001 Paris
Tel.: 01 42 33 43 30 Fax: 01 42 33 43 19
GALERIE CHANTAL KIENER
138, rue Saint-Honoré
75001 Paris
Tel.: 01 42 60 59 00 Fax: 01 42 60 57 00

19th- and 20th-century sculpture
UNIVERS DU BRONZE
27-29, rue de Penthièvre
75008 Paris
Tel.: 01 42 56 50 30 Fax: 01 42 89 69 85

20th-century sculpture
GALERIE PIERRE-MICHEL DUMONTEIL
38, rue de l'Université 75007 Paris
Tel.: 01 42 61 23 38 Fax: 01 42 61 14 61

"Puces" of Saint-Ouen

PIERRE BAZALGUES
Curiosities, fantastic art
Marché Paul-Bert, alley 4, stand 211
Tel.: 06 13 26 53 30

NICOLAS DENIS AND MATTHIAS JOUSSE
1970s artist and designer furniture
Marché Paul-Bert, alley 4, stand 180
Tel.: 01 44 24 04 84

OLIVIER DEBOSCKER
20th-century decoration
Marché Paul-Bert, alley 5, stand 204 bis
Tel.: 06 12 97 55 91

DE TEMPS EN TEMPS
Decorative arts
Marché Paul-Bert, alley 2, stand 119
Tel.: 01 40 11 00 51

H. P. ANTIQUITÉS
(Élisabeth Hervé, Marc-Antoine Patissier)
19th- and 20th-century decorative arts
Marché Paul-Bert, alley 2, stands 131, 133
Tel.: 01 40 11 94 09 Fax: 01 45 35 44 54

ÉRIC LOMBARD
20th-century furniture
Marché Serpette, alley 6, stand 2
Tel.: 01 40 11 73 43

CATHERINE MILLANT
18th to 20th-century decorative arts
Marché Paul-Bert, alley 4, stand 219-221
Tel.: 01 40 11 87 83

LA PETITE MAISON
(Stéphane Olivier)
19th century, curiosities
10, rue Paul-Bert
Tel.: 01 40 10 56 69

STAND 89
(Alban Trehet et Stéphane Danant)
1950-1980's furniture, lights,
French ceramics
Marché Paul-Bert, alley 6, stand 89
Tel.: 06 12 58 13 94 / 06 86 48 60 70

VINGTIÈME SIÈCLE
(Bruno Ract-Madoux)
1950-1970's furniture
Marché Paul-Bert, alley 6, stand 93
Tel./Fax: 01 49 45 11 09

FÉLIX MARCILHAC

ALAIN DEMACHY

PATRICK SEGUIN AND PHILIPPE JOUSSE

PIERRE PASSEBON

Bibliography

GENERAL BIBLIOGRAPHY

Alcouffe, Daniel, *Le Mobilier du musée du Louvre,* vol.1, Moyen Âge, Renaissance, XVIIIe-XIXe siècle, ébénisterie, Dijon, Faton, 1993.

Bertrand-Dorléac, Laurence (ed.), *Le Commerce de l'Art de la Renaissance à nos jours,* Paris, La Manufacture, 1992.

Blanc, Charles, *Le Trésor de la curiosité tiré des catalogues de vente avec une lettre à l'auteur sur la curiosité par le comte A. N. Thibaudeau,* 2 vol., Paris, Renouard, 1868.

Bonnaffé, Edmond, *Le Commerce de la curiosité,* Paris, 1895.

Donateurs du Louvre, Les, cavol. exp., musée du Louvre, Paris, RMN, 1989.

Guide Emer. Le guide de l'antiquaire, de l'amateur d'art et du bibliophile, Paris, Guide Emer, 1st ed. 1948-1949 (produced every other year in odd years, in 4 vol.).

Haskell, Francis, *Rediscoveries in Art: Some Aspects of Taste, Fashion and Collecting in England and France,* Oxford, Phaidon Press, 1976.

Lugt, Frits, *Répertoire des catalogues de ventes publiques intéressant l'art ou la curiosité...,* vol. I (1600-1825), 1938; vol. II (1826-1860), 1953; vol. III (1861-1900), 1964; vol. IV (1901-1925), 1987, The Hague.

Pallot, Bill G. B., *L'Art du siège au XVIIIe siècle en France,* Paris, A.C.R.-Gismondi, 1987.

Le Mobilier du musée du Louvre, vol. II, Sièges et consoles (menuiserie), XVIIe-XVIIIe siècles, Dijon, Faton, 1993.

Reitlinger, Gerald, *The Economics of taste. The Rise and Fall of Picture Prices, 1760-1960,* 3 vols., London, Barrie et Rockliffe, 1961,1963 and 1970.

PRE-REVOLUTIONARY PERIOD

Almanach des bâtiments, Paris, 1771-1789.

Boutique du bijoutier, La, satire dramatique, anonymous, London and Paris, 1757.

Black, J., *Natural and Necessary Enemies: Anglo-French Relations in the 18th century,* London, Duckworth, 1986.

Cartwright, M. T., "Diderot's Connoisseurship: Ethics and Aesthetics of the Art Trade," in *Studies in 18th century culture,* no. 10, London, 1980.

Cole, William, *A Journal of My Journey to Paris in the Year 1765,* London, Constable and Co., 1931.

Corrozet, G., *Les Antiquitez, histoires et singularitez de Paris, ville capitale du royaume de France...,* Paris, 1550.

Courajod, Louis, *Livre-journal de Lazare Duvaux, marchand-bijoutier ordinaire du roi 1748-1758,* Paris, 1872 (re-published by De Nobele, 2 vols., Paris, 1965).

Davillier, Charles, *Le Cabinet du duc d'Aumont* (catalog of the sale of the Duke of Aumont's estate), Paris, Aubry, 1870.

Des Essarts, Nicolas-Toussaint called Le Moyne, *Dictionnaire universel de police,* Paris, Moutard, 8 vol., 1786-1790.

Duplessis, Georges, *Les Ventes de tableaux, dessins, estampes et objets d'art au XVIIe-XVIIIe siècles,* Paris, Rapilly, 1874.

Duverger, E., "Réflexions sur le commerce de l'art au XVIIIe siècle", in *XXVI International Congress of the History of Art,* vol. 3, Berlin, 1967.

Edwards, Jolyon, *Alexandre-Joseph Paillet. Expert et marchand de tableaux à la fin du XVIIIe siècle,* Paris, Arthena, 1996.

Émile-Male, Gilberte, "Jean-Baptiste-Pierre Lebrun. Son rôle dans l'histoire de la restauration des tableaux du Louvre", in *Mémoires de la Fédération des sociétés historiques et archéologiques de Paris et de l'Île-de-France,* vol. 8 (1956), Paris, 1957.

Fox, R. and **Turner,** A., "Luxury Trades and Consumerism in Ancien Regime Paris," in *Studies in the Skilled Workforce,* Oxford, 1996.

Franklin, A., *Dictionnaire historique des arts, métiers et professions exercés dans Paris depuis le XIIIe siècle,* Paris, H. Welter, 1906.

La Vie d'autrefois: arts et métiers, modes, mœurs, usages des Parisiens au XVIIe et XVIIIe siècle d'après des documents originaux, Paris, 1889.

Freyberger, Ronald, "18th century French furniture from Hamilton Palace," in *Apollo,* London, 1981.

Laurens, Annie-France et **Pomian,** Kryzsztof (dir.), *La Collection d'antiquités aux XVIIIe et XIXe siècles,* Paris, EHESS, n° 86, 1992.

Lemonnier, Patricia, "Les Julliot: histoire d'une dynastie prospère de marchands merciers," in *L'Estampille-L'Objet d'Art,* no. 229, Paris, October, 1989.

Lespinasse, René de, *Les Métiers et Corporations de la ville de Paris,* 2 vols., Paris, 1892.

M., *La Confession publique du brocanteur. Aventure extraordinaire arrivée au mois de novembre 1769 sur un vaisseau parti de l'Amérique pour Saint-Malo et rapportée fidellement par M***,* Amsterdam, 1776.

Mazel, Geneviève, "1777: la vente Randon de Boisset et le marché de l'art au XVIIIe siècle," in *L'Estampille,* no. 202, Paris, 1987.

Mc Kendrick, Neil, **Brewer,** George and **Plumb,** John Harold, *The Birth of a Consumer Society. The commercialization of 18th-century England,* Hutchinson, London, 1983.

Pomian, Kryzsztof, *Collectionneurs, amateurs et curieux Paris-Venise: XVIe-XVIIIe siècle,* Paris, Gallimard, 1987.

"Marchands, connaisseurs et curieux à Paris auXVIIIe siècle", in *Revue de l'art,* no. 43, Paris, 1979.

Pradère, Alexandre, "Boulle, du Louis XIV sous Louis XVI", in *L'Objet d'Art,* Paris, 1988.

Saint-Léon, Étienne-Martin, *Histoire des corps de métiers depuis leur origine jusqu'à leur suppression en 1791,* Genève, Slatkine-Megariotis, 1976 (1st ed. Paris, 1922).

Saisselin, Rémy Gilbert, *Taste in 18th centery France. Critical Reflexions on the Origins of Esthetics or an Apology for Amateurs,* Syracuse University Press, Syracuse, NY, 1965.

Sargentson, Carolyn, "Markets for Boulle furniture in early 18th century Paris," in *The Burlington Magazine,* London, June, 1992.

Merchants and Luxury Markets: the Marchands Merciers of the 18th Century, London, Victoria & Albert Museum, 1986.

"Second-hand and Recycled Goods in the Luxury Economy of 18th Century," in *V&A/RCA Seminar,* Victoria & Albert Museum, London, November 1994.

Savary, Jacques, *Dictionnaire relatif du commerce,* Paris, 1777.

Dictionnaire universel de commerce, d'histoire naturelle et des arts et métiers..., 5 vols., Copenhagen, 1759-1765.

Schnapper, Antoine, *Le Géant, la Licorne et la Tulipe. Collections et collectionneurs dans la France du XVIIe siècle,* Paris, Flammarion, 1988.

Verlet, Pierre, "Le commerce des objets d'art et les marchands merciers à Paris au XVIIIe siècle," in *Annales ESC,* Paris, 1958.

Vidal, Pierre et **Duru,** Léon, *Histoire de la corporation des marchands merciers, grossiers, joialliers, le troisième des six corps des marchands de la ville de Paris,* Paris, Honoré Champion, n.d. [1912].

Watson, Francis J., "Beckford, Mme de Pompadour, the Duc de Bouillon and the Taste for Japanese Lacquer in 18th century," in *Gazette des Beaux-Arts,* LX, Paris, 1963.

"Les marchands merciers et le goût français au XVIIIe siècle", in *L'Œil,* n°151, Paris, juillet 1967.

Whitehead, J., "George IV: Furnishing in the French Taste (the Place of Dominique Daguerre in the Royal collection)," in *Apollo,* no. 138, London, September. 1993.

REVOLUTIONARY PERIOD

Almanach des adresses de Paris, Paris, 1791.

Almanach des bâtiments, Paris, 1792-1798.

PATRICK SERRAIRE

HERVÉ AND DIDIER AARON

ÉRIC PHILIPPE

ALEXIS AND NICOLAS KUGEL

Almanach du commerce par La Tynna, Paris, 1799-1819.

Bailey, Colin B., "The Comte de Vaudreuil: Aristocratic Collection on the Eve of the Revolution", in *Apollo*, London, July, 1989.

"Lebrun et le commerce d'art pendant le blocus continental," in *Revue de l'Art*, no. 63.

Baulez, Christian, "Le remeublement de Versailles. Histoire du goût et goût de l'histoire," in *De Versailles à Paris, la Révolution française et les collections royales*, cavol. exp., Paris, Mairie du 5e arr., 1989.

Beurdeley, Michel, *La France à l'encan : 1789-1799. Exode des objets d'art sous la Révolution*, Paris, J. Tallandier, 1981.

"Ventes du mobilier royal de Versailles," in *De Versailles à Paris, le destin des collections royales*, cavol. exp., mairie du 5e arr., Paris, 1989.

Courajod, Louis, *Alexandre Lenoir: son journal et le musée des monuments français*, Paris, 1878-1887.

Despois, Eugène, *Le Vandalisme révolutionnaire, fondations littéraires, scientifiques et artistiques de la Convention*, Paris, 1868.

Dimier, Louis, *Les impostures de Lenoir: examen de plusieurs opinions reçues sur la foi de cet auteur concernant quelques points de l'histoire de l'art*, Paris, 1903.

Fierro, Alfred (ed.), *Patrimoine parisien: 1789-1799: destructions, créations, mutations*, Paris, Bibliothèque historique de la ville de Paris, 1989.

Montaiglon, Anatole de, "Vente mobilière du château de Fontainebleau pendant la Révolution," in *Nouvelles archives de l'art français*, Paris, 1882.

Souchal, François, *Le Vandalisme de la Révolution*, Paris, Nouvelles éditions latines, 1993.

Vinck de Deux-Orp, Carl de, *La Place de l'Institut, sa galerie marchande des Quatre-Nations et ses étalages d'estampes, 1660-1880*, Paris, Lahure, 1928.

19TH C. UP TO THE SECOND EMPIRE PERIOD

Adhémard, Jean, "Les Cabinets de MM. Denon, Sauvageot et de Guines", in *L'Artiste*, Paris, 1835.

Âge d'or des arts décoratifs 1814-1848, Un, cavol. exp. Grand Palais, Paris, RMN, 1991.

Almanach des adresses de tous les commerçants de Paris, par Dulac, Paris, 1824.

Almanach des commerçants de Panckoucke, Paris, 1826.

Almanach des 25 000 adresses de Paris, Paris, 1816, 1818, 1820, 1822, 1824, 1826, 1830, 1844.

Almanach des 70 000 adresses de Paris, Paris, 1836.

Almanach du commerce de Paris, par La Tynna (1799-1818), by S. Bottin (from 1819) and Didot-Bottin (from 1857), Paris.

Annuaire général du commerce ou Almanach des 500 000 adresses, par Firmin-Didot, Paris, 1839.

Almanach portatif des commerçants de Paris, Paris, an XI-1807.

Arquie-Bruley, Françoise, "Les commissaires-priseurs parisiens avant 1870", in *Revue de l'Art*, no. 54, Paris, 1981.

"Émaux limousins et collections au début du XIXe siècle", in *L'Œuvre de Limoges, art et histoire au temps des Plantagenêts*, transactions of the colloquium organized at the Louvre November 16-17, 1995, Paris.

Art en France sous le Second Empire, L', cavol. exp. Grand Palais, Paris, RMN, 1979.

Bailey, C. B., "Lebrun et le commerce de l'art pendant le blocus continental," in *Revue de l'Art*, no. 63, Paris, 1984.

Balzac, Honoré de, *Le Cousin Pons*, Paris, 1836.

La Peau de Chagrin, Paris, 1837.

Béghaim, Patrice, *Guerre aux démolisseurs! Hugo, Proust, Barrès: un combat pour le patrimoine*, Paris, PUF, 1997.

Bellaigue, G., "The Royal Collections: George IV and French Furniture," in *The Connoisseur*, London, June, 1977.

Blanc, Charles (preface), *Sale catalogue. Estate of M. W. W. Hope*, Paris, Hôtel Drouot, May 11, 1858.

Blessington, Countess of, *The Idler in France*, Paris, 1841.

Bosc, Ernest, *Dictionnaire de l'art de la curiosité et du bibelot*, Paris, 1883.

Burty, Philippe, "L'Hôtel des ventes et le commerce de tableaux," in *Paris Guide*, Paris, 1867.

Clouzot, H. and **Valensi,** R.-H., *Le Paris de la Comédie humaine*, Paris, 1926.

Chamfleury, called Jules Husson, *L'Hôtel des commissaires-priseurs*, Paris, E. Dentu, 1867.

De Versailles à Paris, le destin des collections royales, cavol. exp. Mairie du 5e arr., Paris, 1989.

Dion Tennenbaum, Anne, "Le Sanctuaire du pavillon de Marsan", in *Le Mécénat du duc d'Orléans 1830-1842*, Paris, Éd. Hervé Robert, 1993.

Dominique Vivant-Denon, cavol. exp. musée du Louvre, Paris, RMN, 1999.

Escudier, *Sale catalogue. Catalogue d'objets d'art, de curiosité et d'ameublement, dont la vente, par suite de cessation de commerce de M. Escudier, aura lieu en ses magasins, Quai Voltaire, 19-23 décembre 1846*, Paris.

Français peints par eux-mêmes, Les, cavol. exp. Musée d'Orsay, Paris, RMN, 1993.

Gautier, Théophile, "Vente du mobilier de M. Victor Hugo," in *La Presse*, Paris, June 7, 1852.

"Victor Hugo," in *La Presse*, Paris, June 7, 1852.

Gloire de Victor Hugo, La, cavol. exp. Grand Palais, Paris, 1985-1986.

Gothique retrouvé avant Viollet-le-Duc, Le, cavol. exp. Hôtel de Sully, Paris, Caisse nationale des monuments historiques et des sites, 1979.

Guillaumin, Paul, *Drouot hier et aujourd'hui*, Paris, L'Amateur, 1986.

Hugo, Victor, *Guerre aux démolisseurs*, Paris, PUF, 1997.

Catalogue de vente. Mobilier, objets d'art et de curiosité, pour cause de départ de M. Victor Hugo, rue de la Tour-d'Auvergne, no. 37, June 8-9, Paris, 1852.

Jamar, *Sale catalogue. Catalogue d'objets d'art et de haute curiosité dont la vente aura lieu après cessation de commerce de Mme V. Jamar, rue des Jeuneurs, December 16-18*, Paris, 1945.

Janin, Jules, *Un Hiver à Paris*, Paris, L. Curmer, 1843.

Jarry, P., *Le Dernier Logis de Balzac*, Paris, S. Kra, 1924.

Kreisser, *Sale catalogue. Objets d'ameublement et de curiosités diverses*, Paris, 1863.

Laking, Guy Francis, *Catalogue of the European Armour and Arms in the Wallace Collection at Hertford House*, Her Majesty's Stationery Office, 1901.

Ledoux-Lebard, Denise, *Les Ébénistes du XIXᵉ siècle, 1795-1889, leurs œuvres et leurs marques*, Paris, 1984.

Leribault, Christophe, *Les Anglais à Paris au XIXᵉ siècle*, Musée Carnavalet, Paris, 1994.

Martin-Fugier, Anne, *La Vie élégante ou la formation du tout-Paris, 1815-1848*, Paris, Fayard, 1990.

Meyer, Daniel, "L'Ameublement de la chambre de Louis XIV à Versailles de 1701 à nos jours," in *Gazette des Beaux-Arts*, Feburary, 1989.

"L'Ameublement des petits appartements de la reine à Versailles sous Louis-Philippe," in *Antologia di Belli Arti*, no. 31-32, 1987.

"Mobilier de Versailles: le choix de Louis-Philippe," in *L'Estampille*, September, 1993.

Miquel, Pierre, *Art et argent : 1800-1900*, Paris, La Martinelle, 1987.

Monbro, *Sale catalogue. Decorative Property*. Phillips, London, June 27 and 29 1850.

Catalogue de vente. Objets d'art et d'ameublement suite à l'expropriation du 18 de la rue Basse-du-Rempart, Paris, December 12-17, 1859.

Moureau, F., "Denon collectionneur," in *Vivant-Denon*, colloquium at Chalon-sur-Saône, March 22, 1997.

Prévost-Marcilhacy, Pauline, *Les*

PIERRE, MAURICE AND MARC SEGOURA

AKKO VAN ACKER

JEAN-MARIE ROSSI

BERNARD AND BENJAMIN STEINITZ

Rothschild: bâtisseurs et mécènes, Paris, Flammarion, 1995.

Roussel, *Sale catalogue. Catalogue d'objets d'art et de hautes curiosités dont la vente aura lieu, rue des Jeuneurs, par cessation de commerce de Mademoiselle Roussel.* Paris, 10 au February 13, 1845.

Saisselin, Rémy Gilbert, *Bricabracomania: the Bourgeois and the Bibelot,* London, Thames and Hudson, 1985.

Samoyault-Verlet, Colombe, "L'Ameublement des palais royaux sous la monarchie de Juillet", *in Un Âge d'or des arts décoratifs, 1814-1848*, cavol. exp., Paris, RMN, 1991.

Château de Fontainebleau. Musée Napoléon Ier, Musée nationaux, 1986.

"Du style 'à la cathédrale' au mobilier néo-gothique (d'après les achats de la famille royale entre 1815 et 1848)," *in Hommage à Hubert Landais*, Paris, Blanchard, 1987.

Sauzay, Alexandre, *Musée Impérial du Louvre. Catalogue du musée Sauvageot*, Paris, 1861.

Séchan, *Sale catalogue. Vente d'anciens meubles en bois sculpté des époques Louis XIII to Louis XVI dans l'atelier de celui-ci, 10, rue de Turgovol.* Paris, 1863.

Wainwright, Clive, *The Romantic Interior: the British Collector at Home, 1750-1850*, New Haven, Yale University Press, 1989.

THE THIRD REPUBLIC

Bautier, Anne-Marie and **Robert,** Henri, "Nélie Jacquemart-André, artiste, collectionneuse, mécène ou la passion de l'œuvre d'art," *in Gazette des Beaux-Arts*, February, 1995.

Beurdeley, Michel, *Edmond de Goncourt chez lui*, Nancy, Presses universitaires de Nancy, 1991.

Bonnaffé, Edmond, *Causeries sur l'art et la curiosité*, Paris, 1878.

La Collection Spitzer, 5 vols., Paris, 1891.

Le Musée Spitzer, Paris, Imprimerie de l'art, 1890.

Behrman, Samuel Nathaniel, *Duveen*, New York, Random House, 1952.

Castellane, Boni de, *L'Art d'être pauvre. Mémoires*, Paris, G. Crès et Cie, 1925.

Comment j'ai découvert l'Amérique. Mémoires, Paris, G. Crès et Cie, 1914.

Duveen, James H., *The Rise of the House of Duveen*, New York, A. A. Knopf, 1957.

Eudel, Paul, *L'Hôtel Drouot et la curiosité en 1882*, 8 vol., Paris, Charpentier, 1882-1889.

Goncourt, Jules et Edmond de, "Itinéraire de brocante", *in Paris*, Paris, December 15, 1852.

Journal. Mémoires de la vie littéraire (1851-1896), 3 vol., Paris, Robert Laffont, "Bouquins", 1989.

La Maison d'un artiste, 2 vol., Paris, 1881.

Hackenbroch, Yvonne, *Reinhold, Vasters, Goldsmiths*, cavol. exp. *Metropolitan Museum of Art*, 1986.

Launay, Elisabeth, "Le dernier grenier où l'on cause, chez Edmond de Goncourt à Auteuil," *in Monuments historiques*, n° 1995, March, 1995.

Les Frères Goncourt collectionneurs de dessins, Paris, Arthéna, 1991.

Ledoux-Lebard, Denise, *Les ébénistes du XIXᵉ siècle : 1795-1889: leurs œuvres et leurs marques*, Paris, L'Amateur, 1984.

"La Liquidation des objets d'art provenant de la succession de l'impératrice Joséphine à Malmaison", *in Archives de l'art français*, no. 22, 1950-1957, Paris.

"A Notable Collection of Furniture (Marmottan)," *Apollo*, no. 172, London, June 1976.

Mallett, Donald, *The Greatest Collector: Lord Hertford and the founding of the Wallace Collection*, London, 1979.

Mély, F. de, "La Collection Spitzer," *in Revue de l'art chrétien*, Lille, 1894.

Potin, Émile, *Une Visite aux collections de M. Paul Marmottan*, Paris, 1907.

Praz, Mario, *An Illustrated History of Furnishing*, New York, Brazillier, 1964.

An Illustrated History of Furnishing from the Renaissance to the Twentieth Century, New York, Thames & Hudson, 1982.

An Illustrated History of Interior Decoration, London, Thames & Hudson, 1990.

Seligman, Germain, *Merchants of Art: 1880-1960, Eighty Years of Professional Collecting*, New York, Appleton-Century-Crofts, 1961.

20TH CENTURY

Art et curiosité, Paris, Organe du syndicat national des antiquaires, 1950.

Assouline, Pierre, *Le Dernier des Camondo*, Paris, Gallimard, 1997.

Blondel, Alain, "Blondel et Plantin à la découverte de Guimard," *in Guimard, colloque international*, Paris, musée d'Orsay, 1992.

Brémond d'Ars, Yvonne de, *Le Journal d'une antiquaire*, 18 vols., Paris, Hachette, 1962-1975.

Doucet, *Sale catalogue. Ancienne collection Jacques Doucet, mobilier Art déco provenant du studio Saint-James à Neuilly*, Paris, Hôtel Drouot, November 8, 1972.

Eni, Nora S. and **Le Tarnec,** Sophie, *Les Camondo ou l'éclipse d'une fortune*, Arles, Actes Sud, 1997.

Feliciano, Hector, *Le Musée disparu. Enquête sur le pillage des œuvres d'art en France par les Nazis*, Paris, Austral, 1995.

Folie d'Artois, La, collectif, Paris, Antiquaires à Paris, 1988.

Helft, Jacques, *Le Poinçon des provinces françaises*, Paris, F. de Nobele, 1968.

Vive la chine, Monaco, Éditions du Rocher, 1955.

Jullian, Philippe, "Les années vingt revues dans les années soixante-dix, chez Yves Saint Laurent," *in Connaissance des arts*, Paris, December, 1973.

La Brocante, illustrations by the author, Paris, Julliard, 1975.

Les Collectionneurs, Paris, Flammarion, 1966.

Mémoires d'une bergère, Paris, Plon, 1959.

Lagerfeld, *Sale catalogue. Collection Karl Lagerfeld, Art déco.* Paris, Hôtel Drouot, November 21, 1975.

Rheims, Maurice, *L'Art 1900 ou le style Jules Verne*, Paris, Arts et métiers graphiques, 1965.

L'Objet 1900, Paris, Arts et métiers graphiques, 1964.

Wildenstein, Daniel, *Marchands d'art*, Paris, Plon, 1999.

STÉPHANE DESCHAMPS   ALBAN TREHET AND STÉPHANE DANANT   PHILIPPE LA QUERRIÈRE   JOSÉPHINE AND PATRICK FRÉMONTIER

Acknowledgements

A work such as this one would not have been possible without the help and collaboration of those who, by their profession, their experience or their memories, introduced me to this complex world of antiques, on the borders of commerce and the history of taste.

I would like, first of all, to evoke the memory of Philippe Jullian, the first to iniate me into the subtleties of antique hunting and the psychology of collectors, characters whom he has so well described and illustrated in his various articles, and in his book, *La Brocante*. His articles for *Connaissance des Arts* were revelations, and his novels, such *Apollo & Co., Scraps, Café Society* and, especially, *Les Mémoires d'une Bergère,* in which antiques and antique dealers play a decisive role, showed me that the tradition of Balzac and Edgar Allan Poe was still alive.

I would also like to thank, for their advice and their help, Gérard Auguier, Jean-Christophe Baudequin, Maria de Beyrie, Alain Blondel, Marie Noël de Gary, Philippe and Françoise Hamon, Barbara Hottinguer, Élisabeth Launay, Daniel Meyer, Jean-Luc Olivié, Bill G. B. Pallot, François Poli, Alexandre Pradère, Emmanuel Renoir and Bertrand Rondeau, as well as all the professionals who were willing to talk about their occupation, their family and their history.

The research could not have been done without the efficient help of all the personnel of the Library of Art and Archeology Jacques Doucet, and of Josiane Sartre and Guillemette Delaporte at the library of the Decorative Arts Museum.

Sylvia Beder's help, as well as that of the personnel of the Syndicat National des Antiquaires (national trade-union for antique dealers), in particular Marie-Françoise Bezzina, was invaluable, as was that of the team of the Emer yearbook.

The documentation for this book could not have been assembled with the efficient work of Benjamin Loyauté, student at the Icart, whose sleuthing talents did wonders.

The interviews with antique dealers were scrupulously transcribed by Christophe Parant.

The history of Parisian antique dealers under the Ancien Regime, and in the first years of the 19th century, could not have been told without Charlotte Vignon, art historian, who willingly accepted to take charge this part which she knows so well. She also helped us assemble the sparse documentation concerning the later history of the profession.

I would also like to evoke the memory of all the antique dealers who left us prematurely, such as Jacques Petit-Hory, Marc Lamouric, and particularly Rodolphe Perpitch, whose eye and laughter remain alive for those who knew him.

Laziz Hamani would like to thank Martine and Prosper Assouline who trusted him with this book, as well as Jean-Louis Gaillemin, who accompanied and guided him during this project. He also thanks all the antique dealers who allowed him to make photographs without any restrictions, who guided him into their world so rich in history and passion. He especially thanks his assistants Fabrice Fouillet and Jonathan Kluger for their invaluable help.